THE TIME OF YOUR LATER LIFE

THE TIME OF YOUR LATER LIFE

Reflections on Ageing with Attitude

Declan Lyons

ORPEN PRESS

The Time of Your Later Life
by Declan Lyons

First published in 2018 by
Orpen Press,
Top Floor,
Unit K9,
Grants Road,
Greenogue Business Park,
Rathcoole,
Dublin,
Ireland.

e-mail: info@orpenpress.com
www.orpenpress.com

ISBN: 978-1-78605-053-3
Epub ISBN: 978-1-78605-054-0

Printed in Dublin, Ireland by SPRINTprint

Table of Contents

Introduction 1

January: An Ideal Little Christmas 6
            Kiss a Ginger Day.............................. 9
            Who Likes Blue Mondays?.................... 12
            Bolstering Our Resolve........................ 15

February: Generation Clash.............................. 18
            Keep Smelling the Roses...................... 21
            Chinese New Year for Seniors 24
            Leap Year for Seniors 27

March: God's Urge to Purge 30
            A Financial Spring Clean 33
            Mother's Day for Grandmums............... 36
            Puppy Fad....................................... 39

April: April Fool – Wit and Wisdom 42
            Eggcellent Easter.............................. 45
            Bursting at the Seams?....................... 48
            A Marathon Weekend......................... 51

May: May Day Every Day 54
            May a Force Be with You..................... 57
            Take-Home Message.......................... 60
            Kick the Bucket(List) 63

June: Bank Holiday – Sleep Calm and Carry On? 66
            National Cancer Survivor's Day 69
            Brexit (In)Dependence Day................. 72
            Father's Day for Grandpas................... 75

July:	Happy Days	78
	Disobedience Day – Live a Little at Last	81
	Nelson Mandela Day	84
	Birthday Child	88
August:	Chill Out in August	91
	International Forgiveness Day	94
	Carry On Soaring	97
	Summer Holidays – The Great Escape	101
September:	Back to Life's School	104
	A Season of Gratitude	107
	Thirty Days Has September – Cool Ways to Remember	110
	September Surprise – A Love Harvest	113
October:	International Day for Older Persons	116
	World Mental Health Day	119
	Oktoberfest: Keep Calm and Prost On	122
	Halloween – A Time of Tricks and Treats	125
November:	Cultivate Spirit	128
	Remember in November	131
	World Pneumonia Day	133
	Cyber Monday	136
December:	Advent – Let's Prepare	139
	The Twelve Challenges of Christmas	142
	Surviving Toxic Relatives at Yuletide	146
	New Year's Resolutions/Revolutions Yet Again	149
Magical Mondays		152
The Happiest Hump Days		155
Frivolous, Flighty Fridays		158
Conclusion		161

INTRODUCTION

The Thrills and Skills of Older Living Applied Throughout the Year

This series of reflections aims to assist older people explore new possibilities and narratives as they experience the process of growing older. The book is an interpretation of the key events that take place in our personal and social calendars and will shake up their significance with a twist of irony. The book looks at the year, with its challenges and opportunities, through my eyes (a middle-ager who works as a psychiatrist for older people and who aspires to become a thriving older person). As someone who has worked exclusively with older patients for over two decades, I have come to admire older people for their resilience, fortitude and commitment to get on with the business of daily life despite loss and illness. This book reminisces, recalls, reinterprets and explores the themes and events based on a journey through the months in both a serious and light-hearted fashion. This reflects the conditions of life with all its ups and downs for the majority of us. Whatever your circumstances, this book will open your eyes to a lot of ideas and understandings that will change your perspective on the latter part of life. It also highlights the obstacles, many of which are socially constructed, that the older generation faces in terms of reinventing itself in order to embrace the most liberating and constructive stage of their lives. Later life is frequently portrayed as a time of inevitable loss and decline due to society's fear and discomfort about death and the ageing process. Yet, freed from the responsibilities and obligations of the screamage, teenage and screenage generation, and released from the burden of work and the mortgage, people in their later years have the potential to live out their legacy. It is easy to find fulfilment in this productive and enriching phase of life. Readers are encouraged to 'take stock' of their past and current lives, reviewing whether life goals and key emotional and psychological needs have been met, and how this may be achieved if they have not been.

Chances are that many of us have or will have spent a lot of our lives pleasing and appeasing others and deferring the things that we have always wanted to do. Now, as we are firmly strapped into the driving seat, opportunity must be grasped as we finally take charge of our own lives. This book is intended as a pragmatic, challenging and provocative roadmap for this journey – it will realistically examine the losses and changes that inevitably accompany the ageing process, and it will also highlight the opportunities and restrictions that society places on the older generation. Personal growth and self-renewal may only be truly possible when the distractions of the early and middle years lessen and the fruits of our early labours, be they family, career or relationships, begin to ripen. The days when retirement was perceived as the tail-end of life are well and truly over. Nowadays, retirement frequently lasts for twenty years or more – or around half the time period that people have spent in their full-time working lives. The concept of retirement is also changing, with greater flexibility attached to the traditional and often previously abrupt cut-off from work at the age of sixty-five. Many older workers will choose to continue their involvement in the workplace through part-time working; they can maintain the continuity of their core skills but shed some of the more burdensome aspects of their job. Specific skills and experience may be irreplaceable to many organisations, so this requires older workers to mentor and guide companies and businesses whilst embodying its core values. Increasingly, the contribution that an older generation can make in all areas of life, not just the workplace, is becoming apparent with the potential for a collective morale boost during their journey through life's later stages. Older people execute multiple roles as community leaders, carers, volunteers and voters, so their status will take an upward shift as they participate more and become the lynchpins of their communities.

When entering the later stages of life, it is the quality of time as opposed to the actual length of time available that really matters and planning how you can squeeze every last drop of life from those remaining years is the key task. While it is true that decades have been added to human life expectancy over the past century, the challenge is to maximise the quality of life that accompanies this extra longevity. Older people owe it to themselves to honour the dividend of their longevity and to maintain enthusiasm, independence and active engagement in all areas of their lives. The youth of today and tomorrow may well respect them for it.

A Skilled Ager?

The great French conductor Pierre Monteux was invited to become the London Symphony Orchestra's principal conductor in 1961, at the age of 86; he only accepted the position when he was given a 25-year contract with the option of renewal. This is the optimism that is the stuff of legend when it comes to defying the preconceived ideas of decline and decrepitude that surround ageing. Later life has taken an upward shift both in years and status as we now recognise that growing older is a chance to do just that – grow. However, the task of presenting the bright side of later life is still an onerous one as the many negative stereotypes stare us in the face.

The first task in relation to any discussion about 'later life' is to define its onset. It can be safely asserted that at the age of 65, even with the rapid advances in medical science, most men and women are entering the final third of their lives. However, people at 65 may be psychologically and biologically closer to those in middle age and may have little in common with those who are twenty years older. Often, the official beginning of later life is determined by socially constructed norms and for reasons of administrative provisions. Individuals may be deemed 'old' simply because they have been expelled from the workplace at the age of 65 through compulsory retirement, or because they have acquired a pension or free travel pass. Others are defined as chronologically challenged upon arrival in a hospital and their subsequent admittance to the geriatric ward. Some may run up the flag of surrender on the totem of life's cruel chronological timeframe by accepting the norms imposed by others and succumbing to all that bridge and bingo.

The essence of optimal or active ageing is to continue displaying enthusiasm for life whilst continuing to be creative and productive. Role models of celebrated agers include Jane Fonda, who as well as being active in Hollywood's acting community at the age of 81, produced her last exercise DVD at the age of 77. The artist Claude Monet continued to paint his famous *Water Lilies* series until the age of 79, despite suffering from cataracts! Frank Lloyd Wright designed the futuristic Guggenheim Museum in New York at the age of 76 and remained occupied with the project until his death at the age of 91. Nelson Mandela became President of South Africa at 75, while Winston Churchill became Prime Minister of the United Kingdom at 65, and again at 76; upon his retirement from politics he reactivated an alternative career as a writer and journalist. These figures are remarkable for choosing not to surrender to the social constructs of what older people 'should' be doing. You do not need to be outrageous or controversial but simply choose to maintain continuity with your talent while being receptive to new experiences and opportunities. The inner demons so many of us live with may encourage us to simply give up if we haven't dazzled at every endeavour, yet like the role models we admire, we can create a new idea of what the next years are for and continue to be invigorated and stimulated by life.

The counsel of later years may be a useful instructor when it comes to dealing with a national crisis where qualities of leadership and experience are required. The Irish electorate undoubtedly preferred the wise and unflappable 71-year-old version of former finance minister Michael Noonan, who guided Ireland through the recent economic crisis, compared to his younger dogmatic persona who was embroiled in the hepatitis scandal of the 1990s. If the darkest hour of the economic turmoil that engulfed Ireland in 2008 has passed, the pivotal turning points illuminating the dawn of economic stabilisation may well have been crafted by a body politic more renowned for its gravelled voice than youthful sinew. In 2011, the average age of the cabinet appointed by Taoiseach Enda Kenny was 55 years, which contrasted with 49 years in Bertie Ahern's 2002 cabinet and 52.9 in the 2014 ministerial line-up. It is also interesting to note that by 2017, when calmer economic conditions prevailed in Ireland, a 38-year-old Leo Varadkar was appointed Taoiseach. Whilst cries in some quarters called for a greater blend of youth and experience in 2011 during the height of the economic recession, at a time of national crisis it seems skills and experience simply can't be replicated. Mandatory retirement age becomes irrelevant in nominating those who have the responsibility to avert catastrophe and direct a project of national salvation. Veteran politicians may also attest to a different political motivation than that of their younger counterparts. Being potentially less driven by short-term political ego or electoral insecurity, older legislators may find it easier to put their energies into implementing strategy or policy for the sake of long-term goals such as sustainable economic recovery for future generations.

Historic figures and contemporary role models of skilled ageing highlight the benefits of active, productive lifestyles and challenge societal misconceptions about ageing. In a society that chooses to push away all signs of encroaching mortality, we are in danger of relegating older people to the fringes of everyday life and failing to utilise their collective and individual talents. Certain cultures have 'elders', yet, as in many western countries, we in Ireland have 'the elderly'. These 'elderly' people may fail to see the opportunities for fulfilment that present themselves in later years as a result of the views of the society in which they inhabit. Older people owe it to themselves to maintain their enthusiasm, independence and participation, and thereby honour the dividend of their own longevity. By identifying and celebrating role models of skilled ageing, be they in the arts, politics or in our local communities, we honour our future selves. Rather than just living out our later years, we can learn from these individuals who inspire us and live out our legacy.

An Ideal Little Christmas

In the West, we traditionally associate the feast of the Epiphany with the three wise men from the East coming to bring gifts of gold, frankincense and myrrh to the infant Jesus. This arrival is deeply symbolic of the strategy and cunning of a wiser (and invariably older) party guest who, whilst warning of impending danger, chooses to come late to a gala once all the hype has subsided and the clean-up has hopefully taken place. Little Christmas is one of the traditional names given in Ireland to the 6 of January, which is the date of the feast of the Epiphany. This festival is also known as Women's Little Christmas because of an old-fashioned nod to women's liberation by males who voluntarily take on domestic duties for the day. This is undoubtedly to symbolically make amends for the transgression of the wise men in arriving late to the stable in Bethlehem, having originally gotten lost along the way! Had there been three wise women, they would surely have asked directions in order to arrive on time, would have helped deliver the baby and brought more practical gifts such as nappies, which even a baby king would need! In Ireland and Puerto Rico, the 6 of January is also the day to remove the Christmas tree and take down the decorations, although there is little data, sparse folklore and even fewer female anecdotes available as to how many Christmas decorations actually survive a disassembly by males. This leaves a strong suspicion that this delicate operation continues to be at least supervised by women. Yuletide aficionados can, however, delay the packing away of the same sparkling and colourful decorations for a few more days before the Christmas spirit departs our hearts for almost twelve months.

I hear many older people expressing the view that Christmas has become over-commercialized and it is indeed difficult, if not impossible, to refute this assertion. This seems to be symptomatic of the distortion of the meaning of Christmas. If we examine our own motivations and behaviours, we will see that we are all partly to blame, having bought into the frenzy of shopping, relentless over-indulgence and consumption to varying degrees. And as if we haven't had enough frivolous spending by 25 December, the January sales threaten to reactivate the gladiatorial spectacle of pensioners hunting in packs for bargains; the sales are also a legitimate opportunity for savvy shoppers to stretch the value of gift cards or sneakily exchange any unwanted gifts. Traditionally, Little Christmas is also a time of exchanging gifts, especially in the Spanish-speaking world where Christmas Day is purely a religious feast, albeit one that is flavoured with a portion or two of turkey-based tapas. Older people could craftily claim a Spanish heritage and thereby delay the purchasing of their Christmas gifts until the January sales, preventing even bigger holes appearing in their hard-earned savings. Whereas younger folk may clamour for the latest HD-smart TV, Nike runners or other designer accoutrements, it frequently falls on the older generations to endorse that which is more modest, practical and relevant for their everyday budgets. Although a voucher for a tank of home-heating oil may not do much for the environment and isn't exactly a gift that exudes glamour, it is infinitely more pragmatic than the latest espresso maker. By the 6 of January, the new year has firmly arrived, which prompts wise reflection on the folly of Christmas haste and chase, although pious pledges to absorb and implement the real meaning of next year's Christmas usually follow the wrapping paper into the recycling bin.

The inherent beauty of Little Christmas lies in the fact that although life has gotten back to some semblance of normality, it is still a time of celebration and spiritual significance, with that in-built justification for allowing the holly and ivy to linger a little longer. Grandchildren return to school and grandparents are released from the endless games of scrabble and the scramble to buy supplies of oversized batteries for all those toys and gadgets whose operation will surely have been worked out by now. The real reason that Little Christmas stands out from the other twelve days must surely be to remind everyone that Christmas is an entire season, not just one day. Christmas is, after all, more than just a period of the year to be endured in spite of the malignant consumerism. It remains the world's greatest holiday; it is the start of a long-overdue rest for many, not least because of the obligatory trips to shopping malls where retirees and workers alike wield credit cards in pursuit of gifts that make them, if not their more discerning recipients, feel better. Little Christmas is the encore to the main act of Christmas when the best elements of the big feast are repeated with a final flourish without the acute dangers to our heath (general stress, repeated over-indulgence or episodes of intoxication that merit a liver transplant when the twelve-day festival is over). A lifetime's journey along the lanes and motorways of life, with all the attendant potholes and obstacles, is perhaps necessary to really appreciate the true meaning of Christmas: to observe and uphold the true value of family and friends, to re-forge bonds, touch the lives of others and make people feel loved, appreciated and joyful.

If we can slow down and enjoy the celebrations (and slow down we may need to do as we grow older), we can learn to pace ourselves amidst the festive madness that may surround us, thereby pausing to renew, recharge and reflect more deeply. Time will then seem to drain away with a little less velocity. Little Christmas reminds us that the word 'holiday' should not be a contradiction in terms for those who tend to exhaust themselves as a result of numerous domestic commitments. While it is said to be unlucky to take down the Christmas decorations before the 6 of January, wise men of all ages should dismantle their expectations of limiting their contribution to Christmas to merely carving the turkey. Equal shares of the workload will see more of us living and even imbibing, guilt-free, in the Christmas spirit throughout the year.

Kiss a Ginger Day

On 12 January every year we should become alert to the needed participation in an event for those of a ginger pigmentary disposition. Kiss a Ginger Day began in 2009 when Derek Forgie set up a Facebook group intended as a karmic counter-event to the 2008 'Kick a Ginger Campaign'. This obnoxious internet edict saw numerous ginger children assaulted at school, stirring outrage and condemnation, which resulted in the unofficial dedication of 12 January to the peaceful activity aimed at the ginger population. Alas, older people, who may feel similarly cosmetically marginalised, do not have a corresponding 'Kiss a Silver Day' or 'Kiss a Wrinkle-Wearer Day'. However, they may be uniquely equipped to console and spread ginger love amongst the 2 percent of the world's population who are born red-headed. The truth is that older people and redheads, both equally unappreciated autumn-tressed bombshells, have often suffered ridicule and social exclusion because of their observable appearance. Are there any advantages, however, in flaunting crimson hair when it comes to navigating the cruel world of teasing and taunting, particularly when it comes to the process of growing older?

Whilst in the past, ginger colouring has come with some serious downsides, from playground bullying to endless carrot-top jokes, there are also several little-known but not insignificant benefits that come with the red mane. A gene has recently been discovered that maintains a youthful visage. It is also responsible for red hair and its associated fair complexion. This is said to confer an overall appearance on red-haired individuals that is on average two years younger than their actual chronological score. Despite the natural phenomenon of *achromotrichia* (the fancy name for the universal development of grey hair as we age), older redheads retain their ginger colour for a lot longer, often skipping the greying stage completely as they fade from red to the glorious spectrum of waning copper and rosy blonde before the silver-white stage. Being attributed a younger age has been a desire for many since time immemorial, especially among the more cosmetically sensitive. With the added bonus of a lower risk of prostate cancer for ginger men, the title of a ruby Adonis may be apt for some older ginger stallions who can no longer be left to simply fade in the shade. As wine gets better with age, so too does the shock of red locks it seems, as even the skin of those with red hair has been proven to generate its own supply of Vitamin D. Whereas once the ubiquitous freckles seen on many redheads were regarded as facial imperfections to be hidden under layers of concealer, now they are veritable beauty marks worth flaunting. The similar perception of wrinkles as latent beauty lines or even rivulets of commitment and authority may be (no pun intended) stretching it a bit, but those who are carefree and creased continue to live in hope.

Retaining age or an outwardly youthful demeanour may be a challenge for many, but for natural redheads it may be a case of once a redhead, always a redhead. Above all, when it comes to defeating decrepitude, personality and passion usually win over the dwindling sands of time. Our wild, red, firecracker friends have these attributes in abundance. Of the many advantages of the ginger disposition, their reputation for fiery, unpredictable passion and possession of a raging inferno of temper can mark them out as loyal friends or dangerous enemies. This easily explains the ginger repugnance for the hot sun – they have more than enough internal solar energy as it is and there is nothing delicate about their complexion or any other part of their anatomy. Gangs of gingers outdoors, sunscreen in hand and in a flash mob, could in fact be about to engage in a riot rather than savouring the weather. Older people may feel similarly sensitised to taunting from oppressive youths who are easily repulsed by aspects of their physical appearance and who stereotype them and deny them respect. This excess sensitivity, which on occasion may tip into emotional volatility and contemptuous dismissal of all things juvenile, can be readily understood as a defensive reaction against the persecuting younger generations. The youth of today and tomorrow urgently need a crash course in appealing to the better sides of older heads and ginger heads alike by employing compliments instead of taunts.

Declan Lyons

Whilst older people and redheads share an equal revulsion to extremes of temperature, there is no denying that those sporting red locks look their best in winter as the pallor of their complexion seems to seamlessly blend in with the subdued hues of nature, contrasting beautifully with their cherry tresses. The redhead intolerance of cold temperatures seems to almost match their sun phobia; as one study observed, female redheads reported increased chill-related pains at 6 °C whereas a sample of brunettes noticed similar aches, but only near a much cooler 0°C. Whist older people will not turn green with envy at some of the climatic vulnerabilities of those rare beauties with fiery locks, they are more likely to be covetous of the hibernation activities of some female redheads. Research from the University of Hamburg has revealed that the sex lives of women with red hair were more active than those with other hair colours. This is probably due to gingers living up to their passionate reputation and colouring, and red being the universal shade of romance. Psychologists have jealously postulated that red hair is both attention-grabbing and has associations with youth and fertility, whilst colour experts speculate that red hair has the potential to provoke and arouse people more than any other colour.

It is clear that redheads are expert in getting people's blood boiling in different ways, and whilst older people may give the colour ginger no more thought than a desire to sip a ginger beer from their childhood, they would do well to remember the natural allies that exist for them amongst the red-headed population. And if they don't, then just remember ... hell hath no fury like a redhead scorned.

Who Likes Blue Mondays?

With the all-pervasive cold chill of winter still gnawing at one's bones in January, it is tempting to stay indoors and build a den in the duvet until the arrival of spring. This enticement may be especially strong on the third Monday of January, known as Blue Monday, when a pall of gloom descends on people of all ages, as if the sky can no longer handle the weight of the rain and the days aren't really days but obstacles of time that need to be overcome. For the young, *Fifty Shades of Grey* is a racy novel and movie; for the old, fifty shades of grey is a melancholic backdrop to life that struggles to move forwards and which winter can magnify. In 2005, Dr Cliff Arnall, a psychologist at Cardiff University, claimed an equation had been created to reveal the most gloomy day of the year. Dr Arnall, using a crude calculation involving debt levels, current weather conditions, time since Christmas and one's monthly salary, speculated that the third Monday in January was the most depressing day in the annual calendar. Add in the failure of new year's resolutions, low motivational levels and credit card bills barging their way through letterboxes to punish consumers for all that yuletide spending, and you have find a body that fights to survive in a mind that wants to die.

As a psychiatrist, I have become programmed to be on maximum alert at this time of year, as if a terrorist organisation had obtained a new biological weapon in the form of a deadly depression virus that it was threatening to unleash in day centres where older patients congregate. Now it turns out that the so-called research that underpinned Blue Monday was in fact pseudoscientific and Dr Arnall's calculation has been thoroughly debunked. It so transpires that the theory and subsequent advertising campaign underpinning Blue Monday was in fact sponsored by a British travel company to prompt people to book those sunshine holidays. Was the good doctor duping unsuspecting depressives to part with even more hard-earned cash, or is there more than a grain of truth in the view that those icy avenues of mid-January tighten a grip on our minds?

I have often heard it said that depression is anger without enthusiasm. By 2007, only two years after the famous press release announcing the onset of mid-winter woes and fed up with being told that they ought to feel depressed, people reacted against the so-called Blue Monday by trying to promote cheerfulness and levity instead. Having rediscovered their enthusiasm and a morbid sense of humour, a comedy club in London famously launched a night called 'Gloom Aid', and a 'Beat Blue Monday' campaign was launched to fight the seasonal blues and promote the good times instead. Dr Arnall may unwittingly have done those on the window-ledge of despair a great favour by provoking a backlash against the so-called pre-destiny of depression. Far from having to be incarcerated in a prison of desperation every winter, those allegedly vulnerable to theft of their own serotonin can now choose community service instead of other forms of psychological restraint that mid-January may offer. It is firmly up to the individual to decide in the majority of cases: whether to believe in Blue Monday and its associated grimness or to focus on the high points of January, such as the imminence of spring, the discounts available in the January sales and the evaporation of the Christmas hype. To reinforce the degree of control people actually have over their own mood, the great actor Robert de Niro once famously said that any depression should always be met with a smile, therefore depression will think you're an idiot and will run away!

When less daylight equals less happiness for older people, what are the practical, illuminating tips that need to be implemented to brighten up and avoid another winter of discontent? For those seniors who are mobile yet light-deprived, planning a 'summer' holiday in the middle of winter may be the perfect remedy to ensure exposure to those healing rays of sunshine. Making the most of what available sunshine there is and capitalising on the daylight hours by wrapping up and having a good walk, especially in the morning, can boost the brain's levels of serotonin, thereby naturally elevating one's mood. Exposure to a light box for those who are less mobile can be a useful alternative. This light therapy can alleviate the seasonal gloom if utilised regularly before and during the winter months. Aerobic exercise is hard to rival when it comes to naturally lifting feelings of psychological stagnation: it is cheap, portable and comes in many different forms, ranging from marathon running or walking to doing the housework or gardening with that extra degree of vigour. When we exercise, a cocktail of feel-good chemicals is released into the brain, and for those with balance or mobility problems, exercise can even be done from a seated position to minimise the risk of falling. Speaking of cocktails, it is important to realise that alcohol and low mood can be a toxic combination, so to avoid the booze blues, a significant curtailment of alcohol intake is often necessary. Remounting the wagon may indeed come as a relief to those who are on the verge of requiring a liver transplant after the excesses of Christmas.

Swapping the negative narrative in one's head and pausing a moment to notice and express gratitude can be a powerful antidote to all the defeatist emotions we indulge in to distract ourselves in later years, pending the inevitable arrival of the grim reaper. Reviewing all the benevolence, good fortune and people who have personified friendship, virtue and loyalty and have been associated with our success during a long life can prevent gloom-laden thoughts descending on us at any time of year. Keeping a gratitude journal can also inspire us to be more altruistic as we recall people, events and daily observations that exalt us while helping us to achieve a wholeness of soul as we review our lives. Although the days of mid-January may be heavier, there are fires to warm us and a sun to smile on us, albeit fleetingly, as we wait expectantly for nature's rebirth. If Blue Monday does exist and serves any purpose, it is to remind us that the good things are just around the corner.

Bolstering Our Resolve

With Fail Friday staring us in the face at the end of January, many older people will have already cast their new year's resolutions into the sea of dissipated willpower and repeated failure. While we may all be sucked into a frenzy of dreaming and scheming about the potential of a new year, there may be for some a simultaneous bellyache and sense of trepidation about the marking of yet another year and the slow evaporation of the elixir of life from one's glass. That same glass may be more bearable to look at, however, if we can somehow convince ourselves that this calendrical unit of twelve months will be better and life's remaining elixir sweeter than the one that we have just left behind. How we mark the turning of the year, therefore, may reveal a lot about our disposition according to the American columnist Bill Vaughan, who once said that an optimist stays up to see the new year in, whereas a pessimist waits to make sure the old one leaves.

The commencement of a new year does not start with a fanfare of light and freshness – we still have bitterly cold temperatures, pitch-black darkness and dead leaves to contend with as we struggle to stretch Lycra over blue toes, if pledges to become physically fitter still survive. Tulips and daffodils are also generally impervious to the pleas of older people to get a move on and make their colourful appearance, heralding the onset of more benign temperatures. With all the struggle and what we might euphemistically call the 'raw beauty' of the new year, it's a wonder that any resolutions other than warming fingers around steaming glasses of mulled wine are made at this time of year!

Yet many older people can see the start of the new year as an opportunity to reboot their sense of living and shake up a routine or two. Mindlessly repeating the routines and habits of a lifetime can sometimes lead to a chronic allergy of change, challenge, spontaneity and the letting down of what's left of one's hair. Weaving the occasional habit-releaser into a new year's resolution list, such as calling someone who you haven't spoken to in years, may be liberating and prevent us from operating on autopilot and crash-landing into depression. Some of those habits from which we yearn to escape can be downright damaging to our health. Behaviour that sees us disgusted with ourselves, such as mindlessly devouring a box of chocolates or glugging a bottle of wine in one sitting is likely to thwart our best intentions and leave us feeling out of control, empty and depressed. However self-deluded it may seem, any opportunity to reason a healthier response to self-sabotaging instincts is to be welcomed. Does it follow that older people have developed robust strategies over a lifetime to tame the instant-gratification-instinct or do they need as much help as everyone else?

Upgrading a new year's resolution list is a task that may be undertaken by older Cinderellas just before the proverbial clock strikes midnight on New Year's Eve. I have frequently noticed that seniors are a lot less likely to make new year's resolutions in the first place as they often use the old idiom about leopards and their spots. This can be attributed to the fact that as we grow in years, we come to the realisation that when we try and fail to implement pious vows to change our waist size or become fluent in Mandarin, we eventually give up making these oaths as we know they're dead in the water before they have even been made. We have struggled enough to know that new year's resolutions simply don't work because we expected perfection but secretly primed ourselves for failure and abandoned the resolution at the first setback. The same research, however, reveals a cunning subconscious adaptation by the sage brigade to achieve self-betterment: behavioural change is gradually built up without prescribing to the rigid all-or-nothing strictures of a new years' resolution. Thus, the goal is unhurriedly achieved in a sustainable manner. The new year's resolutions that focus on doing more of something to achieve self-guided improvement and direction are more likely to succeed than the resolutions that focus on doing less of an activity that may focus on unattainable perfection.

Activities that fall under the 'more self-nourishment, less self-sabotage category' and that don't always rely on wrought-iron willpower to implement can be categorised under four headings. The most conventional new year's resolutions coincidentally fit into these headings: money, health, self-improvement and relationships. Older adults still display considerable psychological investment in each of these areas, despite the glorious imperfections they may have accumulated with the slow passage of years. Practical areas for behavioural change include health improvement, starting a new hobby or getting a pet for the first time. Learning a language can expand the network of cells in the area of the brain where dementia starts, and it gives the person another set of paintbrushes with which to paint the thoughts in their head. Speaking of painting, such a pastime can be extremely relaxing and gently gets the creative juices flowing. A plan to reconnect with old friends and even resolve a long-standing grudge or dispute, however difficult, can be liberating. We may choose to use the new year as an opportunity to 'tidy up' and integrate many aspects of our lives without leaving resentment or chaos in our wake. For example, planning our estate and tidying up our affairs for when we're no longer around is as essential as establishing a budget to live by when we are. Above all, validating the people in our lives and letting them know how important they are can strike the right chord for any new beginning.

If we're increasingly tired of the same old behaviour patterns year-on-year and the accompanying sense of déjà vu, let's hoist ourselves gently onto the new year bandwagon as it rolls by; let's dare to break those old habits and try something different.

February

Generation Clash

A new year's calendar of music and entertainment has barely been announced when news filters out that another classic rock band intends to revive and resuscitate their time-defying brand of music on the basis of nostalgia and amidst intense demand from their loyal fans. To the younger rockers, these sounds, stirring refugees from another era, are definitely no longer hip, and said rockers are in fact in danger (according to juveniles) of breaking their hips. International Clash Day, which falls annually on 7 February, is a newly designated opportunity to acknowledge and celebrate the ongoing relevance of The Clash and to acknowledge their music and contribution to our cultural fabric. International Clash Day is also an opportunity to shatter the collective eardrums of a new generation and to ensure those fresh faces are aware of the band and its lyrical power. The Clash have been widely acknowledged as the heart and soul of the original punk movement of the 1970s and 80s. For others, the snarling lyrics of Joe Strummer represented rebellion, anarchy and the pushing of those cacophonous boundaries to the absolute limits. Many in the United Kingdom and the United States discovered an anti-authoritarian vehicle in punk music in which to rebel against the capitalist, product-focused ethos. The tricky question, when it comes to negotiating an ageing identity, is if it is possible to accommodate the inevitable realities of later adulthood with the demands of the punk-rock scene?

Many classic rockers remain at the top of their game for decades and continue to tour as individuals or within their respective groups, despite accumulating a median age higher than the members of the US Supreme Court. It is as if, despite years of hard living with sex, drugs and rock and roll, they are living testimony to the preservative qualities of alcohol. And what does one make of the accompanying adoring fans? Are the older punkettes deliberately and gleefully trying to outrage their grandkids with their safety pins in situ or are they simply clueless elders, who, like the objects of their on-stage adoration, are engaging in a collective denial of the passage of time? Some older punks reject the scene over time whilst many stagnate but occasionally participate in ways deemed age-inappropriate or lacking in dignity. Other Castro-like figures keenly meet the demands of the scene by continuing their lippy rebelliousness and attending gigs where they have to mop up the blood pouring out of what's left of their brain. It could be argued that old-timers on world tours, despite a process of ongoing fossilisation, are not being outrageous or inappropriate but simply exercising their flair for music and working to remain at the top of their game. As ever, even when it comes to raw and emotionally driven talent that gets imprinted upon the souls of the young and impressionable, the market seems ready to supply this acoustic Soul Viagra. The sight of wrinkles in leather, far from being incongruous, is merely a response to consumer demand.

For the purveyors of sound nostalgia who have to trawl through their vinyl back-catalogue and get in shape for those on-stage gyra-tions, there may be some acute medical challenges to overcome such as plantar fasciitis, sciatica or positional vertigo. Recommitting to decades of reckless self-endangerment through substance abuse may also be quite testing and decidedly inadvisable for the grey and chubby who may have invested in various forms of rehab over the years. Relapsing into full-blown addiction whilst on tour may be good for street and stage credibility but lousy for staying power, particularly when fans demand a refund for all those cancelled gigs. That's assuming senior rockers are even able to hear such warnings; they may be already hard of hearing, not simply because of age, but due to the mega-decibel onslaught of their earlier renditions.

There is the potential for intergenerational bonding because of similar tastes in melody and that shared language which is music. Even though many cool jazz fans eventually wound up as old farts, goths regrew their natural hair colour and the hippy generation went on to vote for Reagan and the Bushes, each generation has the initial right to lay down a marker through the medium of chords about the latter-day dysfunction of society. The late 1950's kids needed their mod music; the teens of the 1970s needed The Sex Pistols to confer fellow anarchist status on their generation and The Clash to exhort them to ignite a white riot. If the formative identity of younger people finds expression in an anarchistic ideology that serves to manage the turmoil of adolescence, does it ever truly dwindle to nothing or can people remain radical, albeit in different ways? Such a development could help shatter the stereotypes of older people inevitably becoming boring and conservative. If this is possible, it really does reinforce the power of the airwaves to effect societal change and to plant seeds of radicalism that may take years to eventually germinate. Back in the 1970s, it seemed that political and social differences were being pushed to extremes; these extremes were given full expression by many musical subcultures. Nowadays, the music industry seems more about commercialism and less about sweat and passion, even though we have the medium of social media to amplify or confuse any ideological message bands want to convey.

2016 was designated as the 40th anniversary of punk, and it is still mythologised and memorialised by legions of older devotees around the world. A wariness of major record labels and their cynical commercialism was also a legacy of the punk era. This legacy has come to fruition today, along with the power of the internet, to see off some of the corporate dominance of the music industry. Whether the original and unpolished Clash would approve or disapprove in their unique 'anti-everything' way of the online music platform Spotify (which is not a support group for older acne-sufferers), plugging and providing their music is entirely another matter. In an industry that can be very cold and frequently fails to honour its veterans, the revivalist habits of the popstars of yesteryear has finally answered the question of when top performers should stop performing – the answer is a simple, single-word chorus: 'Never!'

Keep Smelling the Roses

The tinsel-laden festivities of Christmas are barely behind us when the love gala that is Valentine's Day is upon us, perhaps appropriately heralding the arrival of spring and a sense of renewal. Yet, by the time the menopause and menoporsche have arrived to haunt a household, and having raised children, pursued a career and coped with the hustle and bustle of life, many will feel depleted of energy when it comes to celebrating love within themselves, never mind with their partner. Older people are frequently drip-fed the notion that it's not just their roses that have wilted; they are also thought to be incapable when it comes to the bedroom or any theatre of love-making, and that any effort in this department will quickly land them in another department that specialises in coronary care. How can we inscribe carpe diem in our psyches and reclaim mid-February to include the so-called bus-pass generation and warm our hearts in the process? Resisting the roses and chocolate script and all the associated commercial trappings may seem tempting, but by doing so, are veteran romantics in danger of giving up on life by allowing the young a monopoly over what is, after all, an ancient religious feast day? The following strategies may be helpful, I believe, when it comes to customising St. Valentine's Day for the veterans (and even casualties) of love.

- There is an old saying in psychotherapy, 'Whatever is in the way, is the way', which is particularly apt when it comes to the ambivalence many feel about the 14 of February. Instead of avoiding something that bothers or irritates us, we may be better off facing it. Arguably, practising self-exclusion from any area of life, particularly celebrations, may be dangerous for older people who can find that any special occasion in which they have to participate may increasingly be dominated by funerals or other times we have to say goodbye.

- Having decided to participate in celebrating love and its rituals, we should realise that, as in other areas of life, you can choose to get trapped in the general flurry of activity and preparation, or you can choose to plan Valentine's Day activities and traditions that suit your circumstances. Tailor-making Valentine's Day can provide an opportunity to be creative, mischievous and funny. We can even borrow from other festivals and opt for new activities, crafts, cards and games rather than the expensive, over-priced meal for two or the other commercial trappings of 'romance'. Valentine's Day can also be about doing something that we love, accomplishing a goal or showing love to those less fortunate than ourselves. Visiting a friend in hospital or in a nursing home to acknowledge the love they have known in their lives, but which is now in short supply, may set the appropriate tone if we wish to change the way Valentine's Day is celebrated.

- Ideas to make the most of the festival of love include having a stay-at-home party with family or friends to remind you of all the different kinds of love you currently share or have previously enjoyed. Sharing the event with other couples who bring romantic food and disclose first-date stories can bring to mind those special moments and celebrate the love, faith and patience that helps relationships endure. Valentine's gifts needn't break the bank, and a small gesture can make a big impact. A love scrapbook, a note, letter or box of love mementos will win praise, as will heart-shaped foods or outrageous desserts conveying intimate feelings of love. For those investing in memorable experiences, a trip to the theatre, spa or cinema can hit the spot. Valentine's Day can also be an ideal time for a short or long romantic getaway for those afflicted by the post-Christmas blues or solar deprivation.

- In Ireland, we are more fortunate than most to be able to pay homage to the relics of St. Valentine himself. St. Valentine has resided in Whitefriar Street Church in Aungier Street, Dublin, since 1836. Every February 14, couples attend a ceremony where their engagement and wedding rings are blessed in an expression of gratitude and hope for past, present and future love.

- For those who are marking Valentine's Day on their own, it is important to realise that there are lots of ways to give and feel love that have nothing to do with coupledom. The day is fundamentally about all forms of love that exist within humanity. On reflection, it's hard to feel bad about going solo when one can do so many things, either alone or with others, that induce happy feelings, reminding us that, irrespective of our circumstances, we can continue to love life itself. The most wonderful thing about love is that you can shine it on anyone or anything, including yourself. This can be as easy as resolving to hug people more or laugh more so that most, if not all, of the relationships in your life become more loving. The ultimate challenge may be the realisation that behind fear, awkwardness or the seemingly unkind acts of others, which older people have encountered all too often during life's long journey, there is frequently a call for love, to which we can respond with kindness and wisdom. Realising this is perhaps only possible at the point of maximum sagacity in life.

Quite simply, there is no evidence that I have ever come across in psychological literature that we love less or love fewer people as we age. We can very much remain in love with what we still have, and the challenge is to broaden our perspective of intimacy and let go of any unresolved conflicts and losses while learning from our past mistakes in love. These mistakes will inevitably be made, even during a well-lived life, and we could do well to soothe our worries with self-applied kindness and compassion. The author Franz Kafka once said, 'Anyone who keeps the ability to see beauty never grows old'. If love is the purest, most beautiful human emotion, and the passing of years reveals it in more abundant ways, then we definitely should celebrate St. Valentine's Day.

Chinese New Year for Seniors

Chinese New Year is an important festival often celebrated in springtime at the turn of the traditional Lunisolar Chinese calendar. The first day of this new year falls on the new moon, between the 20 of January and the 20 of February every year. While its significance for Chinese people everywhere is undeniable, does this centuries-old tradition have a deeper meaning for those who may marvel at the colours, myths and traditions, but who have no direct Chinese connections? Whilst older people of all races may feel they share a Confucian-like wisdom, and the honouring of ancestors and deities may reassure some that they will be remembered in the afterlife, the mere mention of a new year in any cultural context can provoke a shiver of anxiety in many at the depleting store of sand trickling down the hourglass of life. The relief felt by senior citizens upon conclusion of the new year celebrations is palpable; they can get back to business as usual and enjoy the remaining 51 weeks of the year. When you've tried and repeatedly failed to become the best possible version of yourself for decades, surely an annual opt-out from piety and virtue becomes eventually permissible?

While we in the West obsess over our physical appearances as we age, not all cultures are so cosmetically preoccupied. In a wonderful reframe of our changing bodies, when wrinkles appear on a Chinese grandmother's face, it is said they are treated with great joy by her granddaughter, who perceives them as (literally) marking a higher status. Rather than worrying if they have come to resemble the dragon in the Chinese New Year parade, it seems as if the senior citizenry of China are more concerned with claiming the best seats along the route of the parade to which they feel automatically entitled. This is not to be overly naive and assume that cosmetic surgeons and their wares do not exist in cities such as Beijing or Shanghai, but some people in Western society who perceive their own body as their mortal enemy, like a time-bomb ready to explode with the scars of ageing, could do with skipping the moisturiser once in a while and garnishing themselves with the pearls of wisdom from another culture instead.

The principal benefits that flow from events such as Chinese New Year are arguably an enhanced awareness of other cultures and the opportunity to broaden our perspectives and waistlines, considering the vast array of exotic delicacies on offer throughout Chinese New Year. The opportunity to absorb new experiences, traditions and perspectives from beyond our immediate environment without the hassle and burden of travel can be very appealing to older people whose mobility may be restricted. If this new knowledge leads to health benefits (once all the MSG-laden fare has been digested) and we observe how different cultures invite happiness and balance into the lives of their citizens, then this is all good. An example of a commendable stress-reducing strategy embedded within Chinese New Year celebrations is 'Chi Kou' or the Day of Dispute, which is assigned to the third day of the Lunar new year. This day promotes reflection on the all-too-human tendency to utter words in haste, words which haunt our consciences later. The Chinese deliberately honour that critical pause between impulse and expression on the Day of Dispute, which paradoxically urges individuals to withdraw from interaction to avoid potential conflict, this being achieved by staying at home or going to a temple to pray. There is little doubt that if we in the West learned to bite our tongues more often, although it might be sore in the short term, practising such restraint and thinking before we speak may lead to less pain in the long run.

Many new year celebrations will be laced with regret about over-indulgence as we belatedly realise we should have refrained from drinking all that alcohol, never mind that last slice of pizza or that half-tub of chocolate-chip ice cream. If the body and mind festers as a result of our binges, what better way to rejuvenate yourself than to perform an ancient martial art, whose subtle, graceful movements render it suitable for people of all ages? The art of t'ai chi is practised daily in public spaces in China, and its slow, ballet-like movements are akin to meditation in motion. Those who practise t'ai chi and who crave the accompanying endorphin rush point to the greater mental clarity achieved by rising at dawn and heading outdoors to practice this art. Any practice space and any time to gently flex and tone those physical and mental muscles will do, as for some older people the idea of doing anything other than sleeping at dawn is terror-inducing.

The Chinese New Year also calls to order that which is disorganised, chaotic and untidy in life. This spring festival is a time of reunion with family and friends, but also renewal, as we are invited to look optimistically toward the future whilst clearing away that which is no longer useful. In Chinese communities, households burst into colour with flowers, fruit and poems inscribed on scrolls. Streets are lit with colourful lanterns and decorations and people greet each other with messages of peace, health, happiness and prosperity. Starting afresh can also include getting new clothes or indulging in acts of personal grooming in preparation for the new year, as well as thanking significant others by giving gifts and reconciling disputes. It's not just facial wrinkles that can date us, however. Homes deserve a facelift and a sweeping away of yesterday's clutter to retain a sense of vibrancy and purpose.

Ultimately, Chinese New Year for the older observer is about celebrating and accepting the wonder of difference between cultures. It is a time when the mundanity of normal life is suspended and adults become more childlike as they experience one of the oldest cultures on the planet throwing a massive party where everyone is invited and all who participate are honoured guests.

Leap Year for Seniors

A leap year is a year containing one additional day, which is added to the end of February every four years to keep the calendar year synchronised with the astronomical or seasonal year. A year that is not a leap year is known as a common year. February was chosen as the appointed month for the additional day by the Roman Emperor Caesar Augustus, who was mightily peeved with the original choice by his predecessors of the month of August (which linked his name to the shortest month of the year, originally having only a meagre 29 days) for this bonus day. After the great Augustus became Roman Emperor in 27 BC, he was so upset that his great uncle Julius Caesar's month (July) had two more days that his own that he 'took' two days from February and added them to August to make it the same length as July. The chances of having a leap birthday are estimated to be 1 in 1,461. There are currently 4.8 million people in the world who have been born on the 29 of February, of which 205,000 are American, according to 2017 data from the US Census Bureau. Famous people born on the day include the sixteenth-century-pope Paul III, the Italian composer Gioachino Rossini and the motivational speaker Tony Robbins.

Leap years are also marked as a time when women may take matters into their own hands as they get down on one knee and propose to their partners. Legend has it that St. Brigid of Kildare complained to St. Patrick that Irish men-folk were far too interested in hunting and the accompanying alcoholic refreshment and far too slow at regularising the situations of their already secured female prey. St. Patrick supposedly then decreed that women could ask the question to procure the male torso and the lifetime supply of venison that it was supposed to guarantee every four years. It was in Scotland in 1288 that legislation was enacted which permitted unmarried women to propose during a leap year; a system of fines was also introduced if the male object of the woman's affections suffered pedal hypothermia (more commonly known as cold feet) and refused the offer of marital incarceration. Ritual, folklore and tradition dictate that a woman intending to pop the question has to wear breeches or a scarlet petticoat, presumably to set the tone for the final union when the act of 'wearing the trousers' in the relationship is more than just mere symbolism. If a man turned down a woman in Denmark, legend has it he had to give the woman twelve pairs of gloves in compensation in order to conceal the lady's embarrassment at being unable to display an engagement ring. It was not specified if a set of boxing gloves was to be included in order to exact revenge for the social humiliation of the refusal as soon as the other 'gloves were off'. In Finland, the basic fine for a refusal is not just four faults as in the sport of show-jumping, but the reluctant man also has to pay for the fabric for a new skirt for the hapless damsel, who presumably uses it to make a dress for her next date (with someone else!).

Free from Celtic and Nordic superstitions, southern Europeans in Greece and Italy often avoid getting married during a leap year, believing the old wives' tales that a leap year is unlucky. Older people everywhere should take note of the Taiwanese and the Russians who also dislike leap years, believing them to be associated with a higher risk of parental death and freak weather incidents. This malediction can only be negated by a ritual in Taiwan that sees married daughters return home during leap-year month to offer pig trotter noodles to their parents to wish them good health and fortune. It remains unclear, however, if the life expectancy of the recipients of this delicacy is in direct proportion to their ability to dispose rapidly of this so-called offering. Older people looking to attend a niche bucket-list event or a unique social occasion that is exclusive to the birthday-deprived could do worse than visiting the US town of Anthony on the border of Texas and New Mexico. This place is the self-proclaimed 'Leap Year Capital of the World' and summons the late Pisceans of the planet to attend the Leap Year Festival that takes place every four years. There is little doubt that leap babies are deriving pride from their semi-unique status and celebrating their rare 'real' birthdays. They are in fact the only truthful bunch of age-deniers who remain young at heart as they can proclaim to the world that they are only ten years old instead of forty. Talking chronologically, for those of us desperate to squeeze every last drop out of life, the leap year comes with the bonus of a whole extra day in the year to finally get our life sorted, albeit only every four years.

Older people who have memories of personally enduring or witnessing gender-based domestic servitude may wonder if leap day was the most feminist day in the calendar of yesteryear, or if it reinforced traditional gender roles. After all, the tradition did perpetuate the idea that initiating matrimony was an exclusively male right; it reinforced the history of courtship, which has been for men to take charge and for women to wait patiently (or not so-patiently) in the wings. As men and women grow older, their respective personality traits and behaviours tend to become more similar, so when it comes to the asking and proposing in later years, surely it is both logical and socially permissible for either or both to take the lead in any proposal? This is surely the best way to avoid wasting time, should the opportunity for romance or a doubling of assets present itself?

Perhaps the most significant benefit of the leap year is the way it occasionally forces us to rethink how we measure the steadily depleting resource of time, and how we let administrative habits slavishly shape our year, rather than standing against the tyranny of the timepiece and the accompanying social conventions. As we grow older, we can slip into a paralysis of worrying about the passage of time without actually enjoying it. A leap year that shakes up our rather rigid views of how time is measured is to be welcomed. For some, the idea of going four years at a time without being reminded of how old they are is a quantum leap of the most welcome kind.

March

God's Urge to Purge

Fasting and abstinence has long been a feature of many religions. When we think of Lent, childhood memories of passing up on sweets, chocolate, swearing and many other indulgences immediately come to mind. Words like sacrifice, discipline and self-denial suggest that Lent is something to be endured rather than an opportunity to grow spiritually. Is this annual festival of self-restraint merely about trimming back juvenile over-indulgence or do seniors have anything to gain from this feast with thorns on it? Is there a grain of truth in the old proverb that a dose of deprivation is often as needful as a dose of medicine, or are comfort and luxury the chief requirements for a contented old age?

At first glance, the benefits of a detox period seem obvious, even if many of us hope to cleanse the body rather than the soul. Countless books, magazines, health gurus and detox devotees also tell us that the process is cathartic and allows us to get in touch with our deepest emotions, potentially leading to far-reaching changes in our lives. We need to be aware, however, that navel-gazing is literally all we can do if we're too weak to even stand up, hence the obvious dangers in a radical Lenten fast for older people. Selectively foregoing processed foods, sugary foods and alcohol, whatever our spiritual motive, will also stimulate our longing for healthy food and enable us to lose a few kilograms in the process. Psychologists have long commented that excessive fasting attracts individuals who want to punish their bodies. The true meaning of Lent may become distorted if we masochistically pursue an excessively restricting fast. Self-loathing and guilt are feelings commonly experienced by middle-aged and older people as the cosmetic aspects of ageing threaten our self-image. Such feelings can sabotage our good intentions and progress as we try to harness the opportunities of Lent in trying to regain a balance in life amidst a sea of excess. As always, moderation is the maxim here. Colleagues of the same psychologists, namely addiction researchers worldwide, have long been perplexed by the ability of Irish men to deliberately and abruptly abstain from alcohol during the Lenten season, which seems to defy all the laws of alcohol dependence. However, while the Irish manage to achieve this cessation to hepatic hostilities and preserve liver cells by temperance, there is no doubt that bringing ourselves to heel in terms of the demon drink is probably the most useful form of abstention that older people can pledge. Their bodies will thank them even more if the Lenten restraint becomes permanent.

Religious motives will be uppermost in the minds of many who slip their unwanted coins into the annual Trócaire box (a Lenten collection box for an Irish Catholic charity), even if they haven't the faintest idea what to do with it or to whom they should give the bulging cardboard receptacle afterwards. Lent is a chance to prove that we are decent people who should be allowed to pass through Heaven's gates. Of course, some of us may be trying to learn the entrance codes to those gates more eagerly than others. For those who sleep uneasily with over-indulgence of any kind, Lent can be a soft pillow for the clear conscience. Rather than self-imposing restrictions on the autopilot of our daily consumption, there may be things we can improve, such as being a better friend and neighbour. We can express our gratitude more, be better at keeping in touch with people we value and be kinder to strangers. By doing less mindless browsing on the internet or watching fewer TV programmes, we may find more reflective time to contemplate our true goals and priorities. Lent can become a multipurpose ritual that allows us to appreciate the rich abundance of our lives and be grateful for all we have, both materially and spiritually. It is only by pausing to consume less that we can see this. Festivals that celebrate over-consumption and greed, such as Christmas, attract cynicism like fleas to a worn blanket.

When we exit the season of Lent, there is always the danger that we will swing back on the debauchery scale as we seek a blowout from the virtue that has constrained our deepest urges and wants. The child who hoards chocolate eggs only to gorge on them on Easter Sunday to the point of nausea has been chastised by us all. As hopefully mature adults, we need to anticipate such rebounds and gently reintroduce our indulgences, both major and minor. Fortunately for the Irish, there is a built-in safety valve to the season of Lent, which is St. Patrick's Day. Here we can cut a corner or two in our pursuit of temporary temperance. Although seemingly contradictory, this well-used escape clause reflects the futility of pursuing any charter to the point of utter self-deprivation and misery. Life is after all about accepting some inconsistencies; if we allow ourselves a few pints of beer or a nibble of chocolate on our national feast day without having to forsake our Lenten vows, then we should also allow ourselves a little self-praise for our humanity and flexibility. It is by restraining ourselves and stepping back from intemperance of any sort that we can truly appreciate the flavours, sensations and reasons our taste buds became alive to our favourite substance in the first place.

The season of restraint is still highly relevant to older people; it is not just for neophytes trying to avoid the dentist's drill. The actor Richard Harris once said famously that the question of whether your glass is half full or half empty depends on whether you're drinking or pouring it; if the Lenten spirit is willing, the flesh will undoubtedly discover that our now occasional indulgence tastes infinitely better after a maturation period of forty days and nights.

A Financial Spring Clean

With the approach of spring, it is not only a great time to spruce up one's home but also an opportunity to clean up one's finances – doing an annual audit can keep the financial house in order for the entire year. Many of us engage in regular spring-cleaning activities like turning mattresses, changing the oil in our car engines or planting gardens, but our hard-earned cash and income flow needs our attention too. Spring-cleaning responsibilities shouldn't end at removing layers of dust or cobwebs. What tips and strategies do older people need to maximise a healthy balance sheet now that one has finally clocked off and can savour the prospect of realising a cherished dream or two? While it may be nice to exit the rat race, it also means we have to learn to live with considerably less cheese. There is little doubt that wealth along with health is one of the prerequisites for a happy retirement; if you are living so far beyond your income that you're almost in danger of living apart, then an act of financial first aid may well be required to map out and pay for the life in our years. For those like me who feel that the subject of pensions is more complex than particle physics and who have studiously avoided the topic during the earning years but who now yearn to become a fiscal mandarin, the goal is to be vigilant about the succession of little expenses that constitute a small but continual leak. According to Benjamin Franklin, that leak has the capacity to sink a great ship.

Retirement has often been likened to a trip to Las Vegas – we all know that we should enjoy it to the fullest but not so fully that we run out of cash along the way. The good news is that whatever indiscretions happen in Vegas are likely to have to remain secret for longer as the perpetrators' lifespans extend beyond the usual days of mischief-making. Life expectancy has accelerated massively since the 1960s and retirees can expect to live for around 25 years. Soon we may be approaching the 30:30 era, whereby a person will save for 30 years while working to enjoy a retirement that also lasts 30 years. Having a strategy to pay for it, however, is crucial. In reality, many people may be better off without the earlier assault on one's income from high income tax, the mortgage, or indeed pension contributions which in particular seem senseless to those younger folk who frequently indulge in instant spending. Retirement can also release people from the investment in their children's education, the need to wear business attire or other corporate strait-jackets and the expense of having to have lunch in the hated canteen or coffee shop. Having spent years being mugged by banks and financial institutions while the financial ombudsman and other fiscal police forces stood idly by, it is now time to look into all those discounts and waiving of charges that you are magically entitled to.

Maximising one's financial well-being may mean some tough streamlining decisions: it's not just a case of hello pension and goodbye tension. Is it really necessary to own a second car? Is that credit card essential (or indeed sensible with all that extra time to impulse buy) or are you incurring unnecessary late-payment fees? Home costs can be considerable, and downsizing may be eminently prudent, yet upping sticks and moving to an ideally apportioned rural idyll or dream dormer close to all the services and friends that one needs may be the stuff of fantasy. Purging the home of unnecessary clutter and selling it or donating it to charity may be liberating and may pave the way for other life-changing decisions. Sitting down with paper and pen to plan one's annual budget or create one's own financial calendar is extremely helpful given the likelihood of having to live on a fixed income. Breaking out the highlighters to meticulously examine bank statements may be revealing in showing those outgoings that are necessary as opposed to those that aren't. Having direct debit defaults on a monthly basis may spread the cost of the unavoidable utilities and avoid the heart-stopping, cardiologist-seeking shock of that annual insurance bill.

In essence, the fine act of polishing can thus be applied to one's finances and not just those dust-gathering ornaments on the shelf. This may mean tidying up on bad credit that has become as malodorous as the unwrapped stilton in the fridge. It may mean making boring price comparisons before ever purchasing a single item or service or being upfront with your kids about Christmas presents and asking for practical gifts such as a voucher for home heating oil rather than yet another fragranced reed-diffuser or foot-massaging mini-bath. However, smart shopping should allow for the occasional pleasure and personal indulgence such as the smug satisfaction of sipping a cappuccino for hours over the crossword while the caffeine-deprived hordes carry theirs sealed with plastic lids back to dreary desks.

Having fun for free and availing of cheap treats can induce a feeling of intense satisfaction. It also gives us the opportunity to stumble across priceless and unexpected delights. Using a free travel pass to discover towns, cities, parks and neighbourhoods can reveal far more about a location than will ever be possible during a dreary and fleeting commute. Motoring costs can be stalled by walking or cycling to places, which will also potentially curtail our health care costs as we'll be fitter and happier.

The writer Gerald Brennan said, 'We are closer to ants than butterflies – very few people can endure much leisure', which highlights the need for many people to continue working – whether turning hobbies into part-time jobs, working freelance or as self-employed consultants in their area of expertise. There is little doubt that an income from a part-time job can be the equivalent to a substantial amount of savings. Choosing to earn it in retirement may be a matter of choice, but the magic in handling all things financial at any stage in life is to make one's money a servant rather than a master.

Mother's Day for Grandmums

Mother's Day is traditionally held in the United Kingdom and Ireland on the fourth Sunday of Lent, and falls three weeks before Easter Sunday, usually in mid-March or early April. Mothering Sunday or Mother's Day is a day to honour mothers and mother figures such as grandmothers, stepmothers and even, depending on their perceived tolerability, mothers-in-law. While it has been said that only the best mothers get promoted to grandmothers and mothers tolerate a lot, can even a superficial nod to the appointed day of commemoration for motherhood negate 364 days of ingratitude during the rest of the year? The ultimate reward for dedicated female nurturing and all the help that maternal grandparents provide may be extra longevity, as there is no doubt that females have enjoyed an extra survival advantage over males for many generations. While it may be all very well to eke out a few extra years of existence and to spectate as heedless grandchildren trip over themselves to fly the nest, it is not unreasonable to ask who is going to put flowers in the vase of life to acknowledge the many sacrifices of motherhood. Perhaps a consolatory liquid or alcoholic form of appreciation is appropriate on Mother's Day, particularly if the offspring purchasing the said beverage is one of the main reasons that the mother imbibes in the first place.

Mothering Sunday can also be the perfect antidote to complacency when it comes to assumptions around adult children, never mind grand-children; top of the list is the assumption that graduation, marriage, the arrival of grandchildren and various other milestones imply the end of financial dependency. Nurturing may take a decidedly less emotional and more monetary turn as down-payments to sustain affluenza as opposed to cures for influenza may be sought by those designer-conscious adult brats. In fact, the more elaborate the gestures of recompense that adult children and grandchildren dream up on Mothering Sunday, such as flowers, chocolates, gift vouchers and even electronic coupons, the greater the possibility that the umbilical cash-flow cord has flowed or could soon be expected to flow like a desert-oil pipeline. This is not to be entirely cynical about the return of gratitude that Mothering Sunday symbolises – but that hefty private pension or vast estate may be taken a little for granted and hints to its future availability may be unwittingly dropped in the midst of the Mother's Day goodies. If one is lucky, of course, your children may be off your hands and may be thriving in the world, having developed an independent, responsible, caring and charming demeanour. They may already be thinking about how they can repay you for the blood-curdling torture they inflicted on you during their adolescence. Not that anyone would want the younger generation to feel even the slightest bit guilty about any aspect of their youth, including the difficult labour you endured to launch them into existence and being deprived of wine for the nine months beforehand.

There is little doubt, however, that mothers are chuffed when their offspring remember to send cards on Mothering Sunday, and those seniors who are digital natives may equally value an electronic expression of love from their progeny. Older adults who struggle with technology can request novel and inexpensive gifts from their kids, such as a paperless voucher for just one non-condescending tutorial on how to put songs onto one's iPod or how to store photos of the grandkids on the desktop computer. Adult children would do well to remember all the toys that were painstakingly assembled for them on Christmas Eve only to be fit for the rubbish bin the next day before they become patronizing about the array of gadgetry, technology and the incomprehensible so-called instruction manuals that their parents struggle with. Grandchildren may be called upon to assist or even adjudicate in these intergenerational scuffles with electronic contrivances, often to the benefit of their self-esteem and their own parent's sanity. As the American humourist Sam Levenson wrote, 'The reason grandkids and grandparents get along so well is that they have a common enemy'. Yet, Mothering Sunday reminds everyone that they are all on the same side and, for a day at least, should be short on criticism and long on love and gratitude.

It has been said that becoming a grandparent is to enjoy one of the few pleasures in life for which the consequences have (hopefully) already been paid. Whilst the arrival of grandchildren can release a truly perfect love, it may also tap into an ambivalence in women about becoming all-wise and prehistoric overnight. Neither is grandparenthood without its obligations, and the unwary Gran can find herself elevated to overnight babysitter who is expected to watch the kids instead of the TV from now on. Mother's Day may help her reclaim at least some of the fringe benefits of senior parenthood by reminding everyone that, first and foremost, a newly promoted grandmother is above all a mum, even if it is to more than one generation of offspring. Whilst grandchildren are often deprived of means when it comes to purchasing lavish gestures of appreciation for their grandmothers, it is often the simplest of gestures that mean the most on Mothering Sunday: a homemade card or drawing, a cookie or a colourful bouquet from the garden. Grandmothers who have the habit of overlooking faults, praising every success and encouraging all the dreams of their grandchildren certainly deserve these special acknowledgements.

There is little doubt that mothers everywhere deserve a better Mother's Day than any of us are capable of pulling off without their help. Mothers and grandmothers are living proof that not all superheroes wear capes, but whatever garment best defines the matriarch of the family is best left on the peg for a 24-hour period whilst the objects of her affection shower her with goodies and attempt to return a mere fragment of her goodness.

Puppy Fad

The 23 March has been designated as National Puppy Day in the United States. It was initially an America-wide awareness day before becoming 'international' in 2012. Founded in 2006 by the author Colleen Paige, the original idea was to focus on puppies in need of adoption, the abuses found in so-called puppy farms and to honour the bond that humans have with their canine counterparts. For many older people, especially those who live alone or who experience loneliness, there is no psychiatrist or therapist in the world who can rival the effects of a puppy licking one's face, or so it has been claimed by animal lovers who are not squeamish about saliva. On numerous occasions, I have breached boundaries of professional etiquette by directly recommending pet ownership to my patients; to date I have not been sued for doing so. Whilst nothing may quite say I love you like cold, wet mucus, are there really any downsides to pet ownership for older people? Will new pet adopters perpetually purr with delight despite incurring back strain whilst stooping to scoop up the occasional poop?

Whilst it's potentially a noxious stereotype to suggest that all older people are lonely and live socially barren lives, there is little dispute that pets in general and canines in particular provide loving companionship. Some older people may venture out less due to mobility-restricting medical conditions and pets, who may eventually be prone to similar arthritic ailments, can be a useful buffer against social isolation. For those who can hop, skip or even jump with their hounds, walking an animal may promote interaction and conversation with fellow dog-lovers about riveting topics such as worm eradication or animal coat textures. The mood-boost that is inherent in pet ownership was confirmed by a recent study in *The Journal of the American Geriatrics Society*, which provided robust evidence that pet-owning, independently living older people tended to have better physical and mental health than their peers who were bereft of responsibility toward canine or feline friends.

I have witnessed personal experience of the natural anti-depressant of visits from a therapy dog to an adult-psychiatric ward. It is truly the one therapy that is devoid of side-effects, and it leaves the hapless clinician to wonder about the cumulative benefits of actually living with a therapy dog as opposed to just receiving a weekly visit. The pet-indulgent older person may even come to pity their non-pet-friendly friends who actually have to pick up their own food when they drop it on the floor of their kitchen. Other intangible benefits of pets, especially dogs, include their ability to live in the here and now and display a lack of future-based worry. Tomorrow may be very scary for an older person, and the animalistic sense of existing in the moment eventually tends to rub off on people, along of course with the odd stray hair or two, which according to dog lovers is the shedding of fibres of joy and love. If physical contact is lacking in the life of an older person, renewing this through a pet is generally good, as long as fur allergies remain dormant in the stroking process.

Having a domestic animal can help the memories of older people who struggle to recall the last time they were alone in their bathroom, which confirms their cat-loving status. Reading up about a particular breed can also be quite cognitively stimulating, and physical appetites can be similarly augmented as older people who may not otherwise adequately prepare food for their charges and themselves will now do so, knowing that any excess will be readily devoured. It's not just the St. Bernard breed that comes to the rescue of humans; the security and pawtection provided by many dog breeds helps repel potential home invasions. Whilst it is usually safe to trust your dog to guard your home, the same cannot be said for one's sandwich, which will generally be devoured as an instant reward for all those domestic defence duties. Dogs become instant family members who, unlike adult children, don't expect an extra slice of one's last will and testament and whose sense of entitlement rarely extends beyond an extra belly scratch.

The drawbacks of pet ownership for older people include staying excessively indoors and nursing an unhealthy level of attachment to one's pet rather than socializing with people. Of the many signs that a tamed animal is excessively and obsessively indulged, feeling guilty about adjusting one's sleeping position just because your pet is asleep on you is an intimation of canine gratification gone mad. Vet bills can also result in a temporary loss of sanity, although of all the pets that are revered by humans, fish are the least expensive and cats definitely need low maintenance when compared to a 'hyper' dog. Getting an animal to take any treatment prescribed by an animal doctor is a major challenge. If older people mix up their own medication with that of their mongrel, either or both parties can look forward to a good gastric lavage.

Tripping over one's pet or their toys can be a definite hazard, added to the irritation of constant urine-sniffing stops when a dog owner simply desires free and unfettered exercise with their cute creature. Although dogs smelling each other's urine is their version of reading our friend's Facebook status updates, the later affectionate nuzzling of those same wet nostrils into Mummy or Daddy's lap does little to inspire confidence in canine hygiene. When it comes to leisure and holiday time, one's canary can seem like an albatross when it comes to finding pet-friendly holiday sites or shelling out daily kennel- or doggie-creche rates that seem to top the average 4-star haunt for humans.

The oft-repeated mantra for Santa-believers about dogs being not just for Christmas but for life, also applies to Gran and Grandad when they welcome four-legged friends into their abodes. Although pets adopted by older people seem to go from the pound to paradise in one fell swoop as older adopters have more time to devote to their pets, the name of the household animal game is responsible and sustainable ownership. All in all, the scales seem to be tipped in favour of giving the nod to endorsing four-legged friends.

APRIL

April Fool – Wit and Wisdom

April the first is perhaps the only day each year when clever, practical scheming is not just acceptable but expected and appreciated. This day for some may be the annual epicentre of humour and levity, which in the electronic age has never been easier to circulate in all its forms to a seemingly unlimited audience. For generations, humour has also been applied to the process of being and becoming old. Older people who strive to bask in the brightest glow of their golden years and look for a dose of laughter along the way may find themselves stereotyped as they retrieve so-called humorous guides to the ageing process from their bookstores or library shelves, such as the mockingly entitled *Old Git Wit*. If laughter really is the best medicine, this toxic treatment seems to have the potential to do more harm than good to those forced by society to swallow bitter pills of humour, containing all those crass gags about incontinence and senility. April Fool's Day may represent the best opportunity for older people to devise or endorse a subtler form of amusement and take revenge on a persecuting youth without the need to resort to obscenity or exposing bare flesh on YouTube.

April Fool's Day seems to be a truly global occasion; it is recognised pretty much everywhere as the day when pranks are played, the unsuspecting are sent on fool's errands or are made to believe ridiculous things. It may have its origins in an era when people held spring festivals marking the end of winter with 'ritualised forms of mayhem and misrule', according to the Museum of Hoaxes website. In more modern times, the opportunity to play elaborate practical jokes has risen to new heights of circulation through the portals of radio, TV, newspapers and the internet. Playing tricks on others is a great way to cheer yourself up in a media age when stories of misery, suffering, depression and general grumpiness abound. It's not that there aren't issues that deserve our urgent and sustained attention, it's just that for at least one day in the year we owe it to ourselves to travel to an oasis of fun in the sometimes arid desert of the everyday. For older people who are on an inevitable chronological diet, with more days behind rather than in front and who are always stereotyped for being too serious and grumpy, a few happy moments are not a greedy indulgence; they are a necessary survival response in an insane, problem-burdened world.

What are the prime examples of tomfoolery that are paraded on an annual basis every April? The BBC *Panorama* programme broadcast on April Fool's Day of 1957 showed farmers in Switzerland allegedly picking freshly grown spaghetti in the fields and is now the stuff of comic legend. In 1962, thousands of Swedes fell for a TV report detailing how they could get colour on a black and white TV set by stretching a nylon stocking over the screen. Sir Patrick Moore, who even in 1976 enjoyed an old-fashioned image, once told radio listeners that a unique planetary alignment would affect gravity and he asked listeners to jump in the air at exactly 9:47 am to experience 'a strange floating sensation'. The switchboard of the BBC was apparently jammed by reports from April's fools claiming Moore's instructions had worked perfectly. One of the earliest historical reports of leg-pulling must have been in England in 1698 when an advert urging citizens to go to the Tower of London to see the lions being washed was published. I would contend that more than a few stereotypes about later life would be slaughtered if the average age of those who had fallen for these gags was ever known. I wonder if the last laugh would be on the older section of society at the naivety of youth for believing the unbelievable, the farcical and the downright absurd? This would of course be laced with earnest concern and enquiry about the effects on the brain of metal poisoning from all those belly piercings. It is the gift of age that allows a person to find themselves in a foolish situation yet maintain the ability to keep their eyes and ears open.

Humour has long been recognised as more than just fun and games; it should not be confined to just one day of the year. Humour has been shown to naturally release so-called pleasure chemicals such as dopamine in the brains of depressed older people. When immersed in the depths of depression, laughter seems impossible, yet, humour-based psychological therapy is an option that is growing in popularity.

Comedy can enhance brain chemistry and help regulate pleasure-reward centres in the brains of people who are depressed and anxious. Humour is also a way we can cope with rising anxiety or danger when events simply render us impotent – basically, we should laugh when we don't know what else to do. Gallows humour is any comic stance that treats serious matters such as death, war, disease or crime in a light, silly or satirical fashion; it is witticism in response to a hopeless situation. Older people, for obvious reasons, may find such humour an invaluable resource in slaying the monster of death and other serious topics. Laughter provides a wily way to release stress and to bond and affiliate with others in these circumstances. Bob Hope, the centenarian and late, great comedian and actor, understood this when he was asked by his wife where he wanted to be buried and retorted with the trademark wisecrack of 'Surprise me' just before he took his last breath.

The writer Martin Armstrong wrote of laughter in his 1928 essay entitled 'Laughing': 'The whole man is completely and gloriously alive, body, mind and soul vibrate in unison. The mind flings open its doors and windows – its foul and secret places are ventilated and sweetened'. Even when the source of humour is not joy but sorrow, maybe the only real April fools are those who shy away from the infectious therapy of laughter. It is such a powerful antidote in an insane world, one which simply yearns to be shared. If older comics do choose to share their wit as well as their wisdom, leaving behind a legacy of levity means their audiences may well love them for it.

Eggcellent Easter

Here we are, stumbling along, waiting for physical proof that the bully of winter has done its dirty work for another year, when we spot a shard of yellow in the form of a daffodil sprouting, confirming the arrival of spring. For those with long memories, images of past paschal times conjure up a sense of new life, freshness, renewal and celebration as Mother Nature conquers the travails of winter and the deprivations of Lent. We should remind ourselves, however, that Easter is an important festival and holiday in our calendar – an understated, more restrained version of Christmas. If Yuletide is a narcissistic, unwanted, vulgar delinquent that arrives in our homes every year, Easter is its more refined older sibling who has the good grace to vary its annual arrival time and quietly check in and check out with the minimum of fuss. For many older people who adhere to a Christian faith, Easter rather than Christmas is the year's religious and spiritual epicentre, when we remember the climax of the greatest story ever told, namely the final week of the life of Jesus Christ. Should the older, more seasoned of life's pilgrims make much more of this feast time, or by creating hype do we run the almighty risk of confusing the crass and the commercial with the sacred?

Easter time affords older people the opportunity to make good on those promises to take more outdoor exercise, or at least to come up with even more imaginative excuses to avoid doing so as the evenings lengthen and the wind-chill eases. Living in general is easier if not entirely easy at this time of year. A certain pleasure is felt as blizzards abate and winds slacken. But what about those post-winter garden clean-ups and long-neglected DIY chores that simply can't be postponed? Reflecting on exercise and physical activity may smack of a post-Lenten masochism, but for many, Easter is all about the sweet stuff, as evidenced by row upon row of chocolate eggs and mounds of marshmallows vying for retail space. Primed by the now year-round availability of crème eggs, a chocolate-based dietary deviation may simply be too tempting to resist, and many calorie-conscious seniors will briefly indulge themselves with leftovers from their grandchildren. After all, there is a limit to the number of eggs even the younger generation can ingest, and older people are aware of their responsibility to prevent the rates of juvenile obesity soaring through the roof. Food options generally are more flexible at Easter compared to Christmas, with no obligatory, lavish meals to be slavishly prepared for returning domestic hordes.

What Easter lacks in terms of secular excitement it more than makes up for with religious drama. This culmination of the Christian calendar in the days before Easter is not entirely for the squeamish with reference to mob rule, betrayal, severe cruelty and torture, yet the torture ultimately bears fruit in the form of salvation, according to Christians. Above all, this acknowledges the importance of personal sacrifice for a greater or more long-term good. Parents and grandparents are perhaps best placed to recognise this concept, which is at the core of the Easter celebrations. The sense of parental or grandparental victimhood and martyrdom which stems directly from a desire to imitate the supreme paschal sacrifice by rendering one's own needs and desires subordinate to those of the youth must be acknowledged. Not that the young are begrudged the fruits of the daily sacrifices made by their elders – they will have ample opportunities to repay their parents for all that food, clothing, education and iTunes vouchers by choosing the best nursing home for them or hiring the most accomplished carers. The concept of sacrifice has gained a noble status for many as a result of Easter, and what better way to cope with and even gain the psychological upper hand than recognise forfeit and suffering as a temporary blip? Even if divine intervention fails to immediately arrive to mitigate the misery and deprivation of this earth, it matters little in the overall scheme of things as reward points will continue to accrue to be cashed-in, even in the afterlife. In many ways, the lessons of Easter have taught the entire human race the ability to delay gratification, which usefully rails against other impulses of the technological age such as instant communication, credit cards and a media which for an older generation seems more anti-social than social.

Political leaders are only too aware that a week is a long time in politics; clearly this phrase has paschal origins when one reflects on the tumultuousness of the week leading up to Easter. Countless political mandarins have entered in triumph their own citadels to complete their work as self-appointed messiahs. Many have suffered setbacks and even political death yet have risen again to foist their policies on a weary electorate who have seen this cycle many times before. The spectacle of Easter seems destined to be replicated in a myriad of ways during the rest of the year. Whatever about the inevitable distortions and deformations that only human beings have the ability to inflict upon the divine, Easter remains an inspiration for many elders and is a highly intelligent, low-intensity feast. If the Danish brewing company Carlsberg, as the famous advertisement suggests, could design festivals, they would surely all look like Easter, with no cards, optional gifts, plenty of spring sunshine, tons of chocolate, and a promise of immortality for the older generation. The younger, tech-savvy generation should not get their hands on this feast, so let's nurture the niche and keep Easter for the virtuous, not the virile.

Bursting at the Seams

An older man or woman walks down the street with a bag of belongings on their way to the charity shop. Nothing unusual there, you might think, but the unsuspecting passerby is unaware that it took them three hours of agonising over whether or not to part with the contents of the bag, as well as numerous threats from their spouse if they didn't, many mental calculations about whether or not they could buy back some of what they were about to donate, and whether anyone would notice if these items were secretly smuggled back to their family home.

Why are so many of us reluctant to part with our personal things when we have much more than we could ever need? We have clothes we don't wear, kits we don't use, toys we don't play with and pictures we've grown bored of. Yet parting with them can seem as petrifying as a proposal to have a part of our body surgically excised. For those willing to recycle, a whole industry of charity shops has sprung up to assuage the collective guilt about our ownership of all the possessions we don't want or need. Having everything we thought we wanted isn't making us happier, and our increasing clutter is arguably both a cause and a symptom of the stress in our lives. Clutter in the form of the overflowing wardrobe, the paper-logged desk or junk-filled spare room affects our physical and psychological space. It can affect every facet of our life, from the time it takes us to do things to our financial wellbeing and overall enjoyment of life. It can distract us, weigh us down and invite chaos into our personal lives. There is an old Buddhist saying that says 'The moment you own something, it begins to deteriorate'. Belongings confer a responsibility and, moreover, if we are constantly fighting clutter and coveting even more possessions, we are in danger of never being clear in our minds to really think about what we want or where our real priorities lie. Our relationships may suffer if our partners don't share our obsession with accumulating clutter in every visible and invisible corner of our homes. It almost goes without saying that the emotional value we place on belongings may not be shared by others, and whatever we have valued and prized during our lifetime may have an inglorious ending in a skip. Little wonder it has been said that clutter is the result of postponed decisions.

The idea of having a simple, uncluttered life with less stuff sounds attractive to many – the benefits of owning fewer possessions are becoming more apparent. The economic challenges of recent times have revealed the vulgarity and superficiality of unchecked consumerism, and prudence rather than Prada has become a mantra, in spite of our political leaders exhorting us to spend more and rescue the retail economy. We have now begun to question if we need that new watch or yet another pair of shoes, yet investing in shared experiences such as holidays and time with friends remains as popular as ever. Experiences last while material purchases fade; if we use our money to buy pleasant experiences, we get the benefit of looking forward to the event, the actual experience, and in some cases, decades of fond memories. Material items lose their novelty, but we can relive memories indefinitely. Sorting through our possessions before we die and deciding on their fate is, I contend, a necessary task. Doing this incrementally and regularly avoids the shock of having to choose from a small number of possessions and disposing of others if we need to downsize when we move to a single room of a nursing home. Burdening others with this task may be an unwitting form of selfish behaviour and living with excess clutter contaminates our personal environment and our inner sense of peace. Our eternal legacy and reputation may be at stake. Having the courage to proactively, judiciously and benevolently recycle in life reveals a good sense of our priorities, which can only attract admiration from future generations.

What good habits can we develop to prevent our survivors daring to speak ill of our predispositions when we ourselves have passed on to our hopefully uncluttered home in the afterlife? Having a default position of storing files electronically, such as scanning that old bill or buying E-books may save on space. If we find ourselves repeatedly stalled by an attachment to a particular belonging, we need to ask ourselves, would we rush into our house to retrieve it if the building was on fire? If not, then do we really need it or would it raise valuable funds for a charity or a worthy cause? Oprah Winfrey has lent her voice over many years to a manifesto for change that she wishes to see implemented when it comes to 'stuffocation'. She believes it will allow us to be happier, healthier and to live more with less. Her top tip is to put our belongings into one pile and decide if it belongs to one of four categories: a trash pile (to be thrown away or recycled), a give-away-as-a-gift pile, a keep pile and a relocate-elsewhere pile.

Giving away one object a day, decluttering once a day and regaining control over key zones in our physical and virtual world (such as our desk, our computer, our closets and drawers) is certainly the way to proceed and defeats procrastination as we begin to simplify our lives. If we don't, we risk ending up as compulsive hoarders who seek emotional compensation from belongings rather than human beings; we may end up de-cluttered of people and relationships. Dust and decay in this area of our life will be a lot harder to repair than parting with a false treasure in the local charity shop.

A Marathon Weekend

During spring or autumn, in many cities around the world, the great spectacle of mass participation in a fitness event is to be seen in the form of the annual marathon race. It is a major event in the city calendar, leading to road closures and traffic restrictions as runners take ownership of highways and byways on the course route. In the past, the majority of marathoners were young competitors, but in recent years the demographic has shifted substantially in favour of older participants who eschew the sedentary lifestyle that is supposed to be emblematic of later life and take on this most strenuous of physical challenges. Do older runners, joggers or even walkers reap rewards beyond a medal at the finish line or are they in grave danger of wearing themselves out on elliptical trainers? Are older people doing all these extreme sports like kayaking, skating and spinning in an attempt to be thinner and more limber, aka younger, and thereby stave off the inevitable? Perhaps they can visualise themselves running away from the flabby, insecure, older versions of themselves toward a thinner, more confident, more youthful personal reincarnation. Meanwhile, younger people seem to exude a smug sense of immortality in the latest trends of exercise shyness and aversion as they lounge for longer periods on life's couch, and in so doing, sit on the side lines while attending to their personal electronic devices, which are more mobile than their owners.

The marathon is a long-distance running event with an official distance of 42.195 kilometres or 26 miles and 385 yards. The event was instituted in commemoration of the fabled Greek messenger, Pheidippides, who ran from the battlefield at Marathon to Athens to convey news of an important victory. Legend has it that the unfortunate messenger only got to say 'we were victorious' before collapsing and dying from exhaustion. The first health-warning for those who aspired to push themselves beyond the normal limits of human endurance thus entered into folklore. In relation to human endurance, it has been estimated that at the peak of our physical fitness, say in our tender twenties, our ancestors were programmed to be on the move and covering between ten and twelve miles per day in pursuit of buffalo and other mobile sources of protein. Sadly, due to the availability of modern transportation, the human frame moves less and less, and even before every sprint for fun or leisure, a mental battle is fought between one's will and an excuse which has to be overcome before we commit to taking exercise. This is not to say that fitness fanaticism or even fascism does not exist, a territory that the super-fit, older marathon-runner is happy to occupy, but at the other end of the spectrum is the mobility avoidance of which a tortoise would be proud. This avoidance is aided and abetted by modern conveniences such as the motor vehicle and the free-travel pass. Clearly not everyone wishes to strut their stuff in Lycra for 26 miles. A marathon race is indeed a lot of work for a free banana and some cheers from strangers, but is there a balance that can be struck where sufficient health-boosting exertion can be embraced after years of pasture?

I should issue a warning that a sudden switch to extreme exertion for those embarking on physical exercise as a latter-day rescue-bid to combat old age can be fatal, as the sudden strain on the heart can cause it to give up the ghost and render its owner to become one. Start your exercise gradually: walking before running and doing so in a low gear is highly recommended. A mere two-and-a-half hours per week of low-impact exercise may be sufficient to derive significant health benefits. The wary should nonetheless ensure they are appropriately labelled with their medical-alert bracelets, their ID and cell-phone, and ensure that an ambulance is on standby with the defibrillator charged and mouth slings ready to strap up the dropped jaws of bemused spectators. Medical hazards for persistent exercisers, for which cure is impossible, nonetheless include being bitten by the exercise bug, hitting a wall, or crashing and burning out of the race.

Finding a running buddy can make the whole endeavour of movement more fun, even if only to commentate or count the beads of sweat that appear on the brow of the earnest exercise companion. The chances of maintaining commitment to the programme are increased if such a movement mentor is recruited, even more so if they are able to convince the reluctant older athlete that running in the rain gives the added bonus of a free shower as well as exercise and therapy. For those conscious of the beautifying effects of exercise as a tool to look younger than one's calendar age, it is easier to wake up early and work out than it is to look in the mirror each day and dislike what you see. You know you've finally arrived as a convert to the exercise game when the laundry basket gets separated into whites, darks and Lycra.

Alternative ways to let one's body do the talking and expand one's social network at the same time include dancing, which releases tension, boosts confidence and improves well-being. An Irish ceilidh is social dancing at its most community-minded; it is a raucous celebration of life, where the most important thing is neither ability nor agility but the willingness to join in. Older dancers will almost never be chastised for stepping on toes; instead, they can expect to be dragged along in the right direction, spun faster and encouraged with big grins. It is difficult to feel embarrassed, stressed or indeed anything except vertigo when you're twirling around a room so fast you're wondering what bone will be broken if you or your partner let go. If George Bernard Shaw was correct in labelling some forms of dancing as the vertical expression of horizontal desire, then ceilidh dancing is more akin to gymnastics than sex. Like the latter activity, dancing should be fun but above all, safe, and as with other forms of exercise for seniors, it should never be so strenuous that the heroic athlete finds themselves needing a quadruple heart-bypass afterwards.

Whether the aspiring exercise fanatic regularly uses weights or just finds pushing seventy years old to be more than enough, many forms of activity such as swimming, walking, golf, tennis and cycling are suitable and even essential for older people. However, these activities should be undertaken at a pace to suit the person. Being seen as a fit person by the medical profession can save the older person from many a rebuke from their family doctor and hopefully will prevent a premature meeting with certain celestial creatures.

MAY

May Day Every Day

Growing older can be felt not only in terms of changes in our bodies but also in our stereotypes and attitudes. The person who is labelled an uncompromising idealist and rebel in the full flush of youth is in danger of being criticised as an old curmudgeon in later life – even if they are expressing the same views! May Day, when we celebrate the official start of summer, has its origins in the pre-Christian holiday of Beltane, a celebration of rebirth and fertility; it is not just a holiday celebrated in state communist countries such as Cuba or the former Soviet Union. According to received if not popular wisdom, as one gets older one becomes more grumpy, predictable and risk-averse. The notions of rebirth and renewal underpinning May Day, however, should imply that this is exactly the appropriate, timely and necessary feast to warm up those older personalities. Many believe that crabby traits and attitudes progressively harden, and if in earlier years we were allowed to be set in our ways, we may become stuck, if not deeply entrenched, in a psychological rut as we drift into old age. According to popular opinion, this entrenchment may manifest in our habits, and older people are lambasted if they prefer drinking tea out of bone china rather than from any old cup or loathe drinking wine from a plastic beaker rather than a wine glass. Older people may also be dismissed as the most deeply rigid and conservative section of society who cling to their views as tenaciously as a corn plaster. How can older people be young and celebrate their inner revolutionary to a dismissive and sceptical youth?

Traditionally, the first of May has been celebrated as International Workers Day, when labourers galvanized movements in past centuries, asserted their rights and demanded economic well-being. My earliest memories of May Day is of a bushy-browed Leonid Brezhnev, the former Soviet Leader, proudly surveying giant missiles on trucks on Moscow's red square during the May Day military parade. Our present generation of pensioners will recall more recent struggles for justice across the world in the form of civil rights movements, student protests against war and global conflicts and rebellion against various military and bureaucratic elites. It is noteworthy that those who barely had their first flush of youth manning barricades in 1968 as eighteen-year-olds are about to receive their pensions today. If Che Guevara were alive today (he would be in his mid-eighties), there is a strong possibility that even this pistol-toting icon would be smoking his Havana cigar on the veranda of a nursing home. The question is whether a figure such as Che would have learned a lesson or two or even modified some of his principles without abandoning them entirely along life's journey, thereby confounding the socialist sceptics of the sixties.

The first lesson for the older generation to appreciate is to realise the benefits of flexibility, meaning that they need not be young after their time or old before their time, but instead firmly *of* their time. It is important at the outset to recognise that older people are not a single uniform group, fixed in their ways like cement. Many people pass seamlessly from youth to old age without making a fuss about it. To them, age is unimportant; one is simply the way one feels and every phase in life has its merits. This group of senior citizens feels no need to criticise youth or pass judgement on any aspect of the rich mosaic of life such as urban graffiti, cosmetic surgery or an unrestrained youth culture. Life is good, they suggest, and if not, then that's life too, but they are aware that they have only one life. For them it's not about relentlessly denigrating youth and seeing all fresh-faced members of society as immoral, lazy, insolent or degenerate. For the flexible ager it's not about predicting that things can only get worse and having the greatest pleasure in seeing their prejudices confirmed. Nor, on the other hand, is it about forever relishing new and exciting ideas and dressing beneath age and weight or being obsessed with the latest trends. The outrageous stereotype of older people stressing rebellion and non-conformity is about as useful as a parachute for a pig, no matter how amusing stories of 85-year-olds using them to jump out of a plane may seem. People may also choose to be stuck in time, oblivious to trends and remain studiously moth-balled in the era when they were happiest, the era that defined them. The tell-tale signs of this may include ponytails, hippy bangles and ear studs.

As ever, getting the balance in relation to the stance we wish to consciously adopt in relation to the passage of our years is the way forward. May Day can remind us to nurture our inner rebel a little, be a little more passionate and principled and never relinquish our independent spirit, unless we really have to. It's not by any means inevitable that as we age the broadness of mind and narrowness of waist change places. Remaining enthusiastic and productive are crucial elements in our survival strategy as we grow older. Armoured with a sense of scepticism, cunning and wisdom, we can remember that although the barricades we manned in our youth are lofty, elevated platforms from which to survey all that is wrong in society, they are equally useful shelters from the water-cannons of time that threaten to dampen our enthusiasm as we grow in years.

May a Force Be with You

The urge to shuffle off the stage may grow stronger in later years, but the energy boost that accompanies the start of summer should encourage us to shuffle back onto life's stage to survey the arena and resume a central role. The month of May is synonymous with the fulsome regeneration of nature and the start of longer summer days, which entice us with colour, light and a growing sense of anticipation – perhaps the opposite of winter's discontent. In Ireland, the entire month of May belongs to the Bealtaine festival, when a range of artistic endeavours from cinema to dance to painting to theatre are showcased with the aim of promoting the talents and creativity of older artists. During the month of May, many services (including even acute mental-health services at my in-patient facility) raise their game to stage creative and artistic activities with a direct therapeutic focus. This is in the hope that service users will acquire a year-round interest in the arts. The name 'Bealtaine' derives from the old Gaelic word meaning 'bright fire', and in earlier times bonfires played an important part in rituals and celebrations that heralded the beginning of summer and the blossoming of flowers and trees.

One of the aims of the modern Bealtaine festival is to make new and challenging artistic work and ensure the communication of traditions between generations. Whether the younger generation are inclined to listen to or learn about their cultural heritage amidst all that texting and browsing is another matter entirely. They may be very surprised to know that many of the standout artistic creations of human history were completed by the chronologically lean. Older artists and writers have a way of seeing and capturing the profound nature and beauty of life, the mysteries of which are difficult to access by those less mature in years. The Cuban-born artist Carmen Herrera, who sold her first painting at the age of 89, is a case in point. The demand for her work has skyrocketed in recent years – a demand that at age 102 she is still thankfully able to fulfil. Surely the best way to launch a real intergenerational conversation is to reassure the massive expectation generation that they don't have to have achieved everything or have every box of life ticked by the age of 30?

We will also do more than slaughter a few stereotypes if we realise that creativity can accelerate as we age, whether our motives are to re-evaluate our lives or create meaning in life. There are many opportunities to reap a harvest of creative expression in later life, if only we can see and grasp the favourable circumstances that arise when we are liberated from the responsibilities and commitments of our busy middle years. What better way to jump-start our efforts in exploring new ideas and making desired changes than to be relatively free of life's rodent race? Charged with a growing sense of personal freedom, creativity may be enhanced by our search for meaning through an analysis and retelling of our lives. Our energies may be further boosted by the advanced and allegedly frail stages of life in our ninth decade, or the so-called encore phase, when we have a desire to make a final statement or contribution – to design one more piece of urban graffiti on our portion of the wall of life. By remembering to always place the mind at the centre of artistic and creative expression, we can be finally free to focus on the further development and enjoyment of our life without the distraction of bodily needs and pleasures. That's not to say that frustrated or unrequited corporeal or spiritual urges don't add a creative tension to art – the work of W.B. Yeats being a case in point, when his palpable inner discord separates his work from the rest of the poetic archive.

One of the most literal definitions of 'May' is to be allowed to express possibility, even desire, which to me is an obvious door-opener that invites older people in. They can make sense of what happened during their lives through creative endeavours by reflecting often and expressing through art emotions that cannot be plainly spoken. Art therapy is now a mainstream form of psychotherapy that involves the encouragement of free self-expression through painting, drawing and modelling. The creative process involved in expressing one's self artistically can help older people to resolve many issues of their past as well as develop and manage their feelings, reduce stress and enhance self-esteem and awareness. For those who have been so-called outsiders during their lives, art and the creativity that inspires it allow others to understand and become closer to them. Artistic activity forges a connection with others and is always a beautiful antidote to the meaninglessness that some may perceive during life's journey. It somehow allows us to finally vanquish our inner demons and leave a legacy beyond the limits of the mortal coil. As Victor Frankl said shortly after his release from a concentration camp during World War Two, 'suffering ceases to be suffering at the moment it finds a meaning'.

The other symbol of the month of May is the mayfly, which, living only for a single day, symbolises the transience and brevity of life but also its freshness, fullness and completeness. The call to artistically flourish during the month of May reminds us that members of an older generation are perhaps best-placed, like the mayfly, to perceive more, express more and thus artistically achieve more.

Take-Home Message

World Telecommunications Day falls on the 17 of May every year and celebrates the constant evolution of one of the most important factors in our lives: communication. It aims to increase awareness, as if it were needed, of how crucial communication is as well as to promote the development of more technologically advanced ways of communicating. The landmarks in communication development range from the telegraph to the telephone, the launch of the first satellite to the birth of the internet. These developments stand out in human history and successive generations seem to herald their arrival with ever-more connectivity. New nouns and verbs have been added to the human vocabulary, such as 'blog', 'Skype' and 'Tweet', while older words such as 'cloud' and 'virus' take on a new meaning. For the last 50 years the Catholic Church has aspired to muscle in on the act of auctioning the airwaves in acknowledging the Sunday before Pentecost as its own World Communications Day, when the faithful reflect on the achievements of the media and focus on how best they can use it to promote spiritual values.

Members of an older age group may say that the twenty-first century has so far been a contradiction in terms in respect of communication means, as we seem to speak less while we connect more, while younger people find it hard to believe that people once used their mouths to communicate and had to look each other in the eye when speaking. Does this mismatch in perception about inter-personal connections have implications for inter-generational communication? Do younger people run the risk of perceiving dialogue or any conversation with older people as a tiresome, time-consuming duty and a 'necessary therapy' for seniors, rather than understanding how it develops and broadens our relationships? Older people equally run the risk of being an easy target of youthful derision by refusing to meet a generation halfway and staying stubbornly behind the technology curve when they refuse to brush up on text-speak, for example. The reality is that parents and grandparents are and remain active communication mentors of the young, instilling the attributes of openness, consideration and generosity that underpin our communication skills. Implicit in this informal tutoring should be the key message that the more time we spend 'connected' by a myriad of devices, the less time we have to develop true friendships in the real world. Older people have a real point to make when they notice that people can become prisoners of their phones, which is presumably why such mobile devices are called cell phones in the first place! Veteran users of early devices will remember how cool the first brick-like phones were when they first appeared; only later did people realise that they were as cool as electronic tags on remand prisoners. Like so many subsequent technological aids, phones have become absolutely indispensable and so convenient that they are almost an inconvenience.

Yet only the older generation knows that communication is not all about technology, and that technological gizmos are not the only barrier to older members of society having their social needs met. It is truly a tragedy of modern living that older people who live a few doors apart, have exactly the same needs and experience the same struggles with loneliness never get to meet. A society that values privacy above the ability to hot wire into each other's conversations and exchange news is well on the way to a degree of social separation worthy of a contagious disease. Younger folk will have a different take on privacy as they fail to think before they post and are left to ponder if their boss has seen their latest rant or selfie on Facebook. One's communication style may well be a reflection of a person's inner psychological state. How open are we to new experiences and avoiding extreme introversion and isolation? When we no longer have a full-time job that provides us with status and a social life all rolled into one, do we proactively attend to our social needs in retirement, or do we lean away from, rather than lean into, social relationships? How we communicate with others and how we nourish and attend to the mutual connections in our network is key.

The onus on the older generation must be to look at their unconscious response to doing something new or different and question themselves if they find their default response is to say no when faced with unfamiliar situations, people or challenges (and that includes the dreaded gadget world). If communication in general is stuck with technology as its intermediary, for better or for worse, then it behoves an older generation to keep pace with it. Like exercising, few older people would aspire to run a marathon in under two hours, but those who completely eschew physical activity and who decline to command their muscles to move may as well measure themselves for a wheelchair. Learning to master a new skill such as emailing, texting or Tweeting is essential for re-firing us intellectually and stimulating the brain – as crucial as oxygen is to a deep-sea diver. If we don't continue to learn new skills, vegetation will take hold in the margins of our cerebral cortex as well as along our herbivorous borders. The trick is to see technological aids to communication as not something to be learned to avoid getting left behind, but something to savour the triumphs of when we become competent in using them. Recognising these opportunities to do things more efficiently can mean a better balance in our personal lives.

Communication has certainly evolved dramatically since humans first relied on the technological intermediary of Morse Code and telegraphs to get our message across. While an older generation tends to bow down to the tech knowhow of the millennials, the struggle to communicate between generations is nothing new, and technology may be a symptom rather than a cause of this. Seasoned communicators can 'have the talk' with their younger counterparts in any environment, explaining the importance of looking people in the eye or showing their sceptical peers that young people who converse while only staring at their smartphone are actually taking notes on the conversation and not playing games. Most importantly, skilled communication is about letting go of stereotypes and treating each other as people, not just representatives of a particular social or demographic category about which it is all too easy to mindlessly generalise.

Kick the Bucket(List)

The essayist Oliver Wendell Holmes once proclaimed in the nineteenth century: 'Alas for those that never sing but die with all their music in them'. This quote highlights how at some point in our lives we may wonder if what we've done with our time on earth bears any significance, a question that may cause us to reflect on what we may yet achieve during the rest of our existence. This existential issue burns ever brighter when our expectations for lifelong achievement and ability in later years come face to face with a reality that may not meet those hopes and dreams. A bucket list is thus defined as a list of achievements that a person hopes to have accomplished during their lifetime. The list is an entirely flexible entity and can be continuously altered, updated and contemplated, much like the person who compiles it, despite the worst efforts of those sceptics and 'dream-squashers' who can occasionally get in the way.

In many cases, and quite paradoxically, the less time we have for our future existence and the clearer the intimations of mortality, the greater the urgency and effort in squeezing every last drop from life. The student preparing for exams understands this fully and will readily admit that their revision is more productive in the weeks rather than in the months before such a deadline, which usually also coincides with prompt detoxification and the regaining of sobriety. In relation to unrequited ambition and personal fulfilment, we have a simple choice in that we may gracefully detach from earlier aspirations and hope our unfulfilled dreams may be carried into our next karmic account or we can reinstate them, in part or in whole, as at least potentially realisable. A wise man in China one said 'Enjoy yourself. It's later than you think'. With life's final curtain-call looming, this is no time to forget one's dreams or the potentially hilarious ideas in our personal script that allow us to live a little.

Many will recall the 2007 movie *The Bucket List*, starring Jack Nicholson and Morgan Freeman, who were cast as two complete strangers who happened to meet in the same hospital room. Although the characters came from different backgrounds, they found they had in common a need to come to terms with who they were and what they had or hadn't done with their lives. Their brush with illness caused them both to realise that every man dies, but not all men really live. In an effort to redress this and render their remaining time more fully lived, the two infirm heroes remove their restraining IV drips and embark on a series of adventures, some of which are downright dangerous and outrageous. Apart from forming a unique bond, the characters come to realise the relationship between the fear of death and the preceding fear of life. They find the courage that Mark Twain spoke of when he wrote about men who live fully but who are also prepared to die at any time. It's no contradiction to state that it may be easier to reach an almost obligatory moment of epiphany during a crisis of acute illness, but what about those who have time to strategically plan all the highlights of activities and goals from a place of calmer reflection?

A bucket list is often compared to a shopping list, but the commodities sought are experiences rather than material products and the act of their purchase is a little more complex than a stroll to the nearest corner shop. The essential act is to brainstorm and create a list, log, catalogue or strategy to get more from the time remaining before we expire. Far from this being a morbid exercise, it's actually all about living. The content of the list can include upcoming goals that are big, small and random. Far from it being a self-indulgent exercise, the time that it may take to compile the list without distraction or the usual flurry of day-to-day activities may be transformative to the person compiling it and to the people around them. An older person who plans to jump out of a plane at the age of 80 may be a superb role model for their peers, particularly if they undertake the adventure with a parachute! The typical areas where the bucket-list beginner assembles their dream pursuits can begin at A and end at Z, covering adventure, animals, nature, creativity, entertainment, fashion, beauty, personal growth, sport, fitness, transportation, travel and many more. Whilst the concept of adventure may seem life-shortening to some, depending on their medical histories and respiratory status, many experiences can be tailored to the needs and abilities of the person. Whilst the dream of arriving in a seaplane may seem expeditionary for some, it is still technically and physiologically feasible, even in cases of advanced frailty (provided that one's health insurer takes a sensible view of mortality and accepts that even boredom can be a fatal condition).

There may also be that insidious inner demon to do battle with, the kind that has cast doubt on our abilities to realise many goals, dreams and ambitions. It is high time, however, to decide that the same monkey who has squatted on our shoulders since time immemorial deserves to be thrown off as we finally change our mind about the things that scare us. In the past, before a daunting task, we may have been so wrapped up in the nerve-wrenching dialogue we were having with ourselves that we were defeated before we even began. Guilt equally may have stymied any legitimate enjoyment that our efforts should have secured. The magical, unfailing technique for dealing with this anxiety, however, is to identify and label it, confronting it with the confidence that it will diminish over time. The same imagination that fuels our neurosis can be redirected to generate a different reality and a different set of expectations, allowing us to perceive a life-bucket that is in a half-filled rather than a half-empty state.

JUNE

Bank Holidays – Sleep Calm and Carry On?

There was a time when an approaching bank holiday was like a gentle meandering stream for those buffeted by the discontented, crazy torrents of life, work and endless tasks. Just as you're about to fall off life's treadmill, along comes a long weekend with the treat of a deleted Monday, giving us the potential to recharge our batteries. The previous worker-bee generation would have dreamed about these precious days off weeks in advance, got down on bended knee to pray for good weather, broken their necks to get out of the towns and cities and headed for the countryside. This was in an era when flasks and sandwiches, rather than airport duty free, were the main novelties. For the more fiscally aware or challenged, working on a bank holiday was seen as a lucrative opportunity to earn extra pay and may have been actively sought after, rather than studiously avoided to the point of pressing the late sick-note button. As one finds the work-life-balance scale distinctly tipping toward life rather than work in the aftermath of retirement, are these compulsory rest days inscribed on one's calendar of relevance or even benefit anymore? In relation to expressing our gratitude for the brief liberation from the daily grind, should we be saying thanks to our banks for the day-long pause in general commerce inspired by the closure of our financial institutions, or in the age of internet banking and teller-free services, does even the term 'bank holiday' seem more than a little outdated?

Looking at financial institutions and older customers, it is clearly an understatement to say that the relationship between the older client and their bank has changed in recent years. Older people have had to experience an acute and then chronic separation anxiety as the toxic combination of hardware, software and a bewildering array of financial products, terminologies and so-called methodologies have

66

threatened to block immediate access to personal liquidity. The devilish intermediary known as the computer has increasingly driven a sense of techno-financial alienation amongst older people at every point of interaction with their banks. Setting even a single footstep inside one's local (or increasingly distant and virtual) branch is a supreme exercise in expectation management as the older customer may feel abandoned, separated from the reassuring words of banter with a friendly bank official and left to grapple alone with machines that promise to do everything except the customary but vital handshake at the end of the transaction. Many an older customer has taken themselves off to their doctor to have screening tests for dementia, having failed to recall their PIN number when faced with unforgiving technology that may punish them by swallowing one's sacred bank card if a succession of errors or brain freezes occur. A request for a paper statement or cheque book by the older customer may elicit scorn amongst distracted bank officials, or even worse, a patronising invitation to try out the new technology at home (meant to imply their children's homes), but only when supervised by the said offspring or in the presence of a digitally competent adult. What's so wrong with having a choice in terms of paper versus electronic, just as we have a choice with print books versus E-books?

In recent years, older bank customers could have been forgiven for thinking the word 'bank' was about to be erased from the vernacular and that 'bank holiday' could have implied the permanent departure of the entire financial system after the global economic meltdown of 2008. The fall of the Eurozone currency and the global financial crisis threatened to destabilise any sense of financial security, even at an individual level, as governments rushed to guarantee personal deposits to avoid the collapse of the banking system. The mix of ineptitude, arrogance and incompetence that lead to the near break-up of the banking system was committed by what one Irish economist called an 'aristocracy of incompetence', namely banking chiefs and their so-called regulators, who failed to notice the risks and flaws in their practices. The lack of accountability for this crisis and the resultant economic recession was startling in itself, but it is indicative of the enormous sway still held by bankers over many societies that is indicative of a power, if not a stranglehold, which would have been the envy of many dictatorial regimes in the darker eras of human history. The resultant economic stagnation that followed the recession left many older people unable to live off the proceeds of savings as they had before, which put a severe squeeze, if not an absolute asphyxiation, on their day-to-day income. The fact that governments choose words such as 'pillar banks' to endorse some of the surviving and admittedly less roguish financial institutions is hardly reassuring to the older bank client who perceives little changes made to the foundations of the financial system.

The recent economic challenges have served to remind older people that we own nothing in reality and, in banking parlance, we borrow everything. Many cautious older savers had diligently paid off mortgages and prudently invested savings and lump sums until the crash came along, and with it the need to bail out their children and pay *their* debts and mortgages. This made the need to compile a will something of a pointless exercise as the younger generation had their inheritance well in advance!

In an era of endless trappings of consumerism, wall-to-wall retail spending, and financial mismanagement in a society that forever confuses wants with needs, a holiday from banking and all that follows in its expensive coat tails is just what the older person needs.

National Cancer Survivor's Day

National Cancer Survivors Day is a secular holiday celebrated on the first Sunday in June, primarily in the United States. Cancer Survivors Day honours those who have battled cancer and won and provides inspiration for those who have been diagnosed. It also provides a platform of support for friends, families and communities to raise awareness of how life and recovery after a cancer diagnosis is increasingly becoming a reality. Younger people who are diagnosed with cancer are rightly lauded as brave battlers, whereas older cancer patients (who have higher prevalence rates of most carcinoma types) tend to fly under the radar or the MRI scanner. In the healthcare professional community, we must avoid complacency and lassitude when it comes to diagnosing, intervening and improving quality of life for older people with cancer. To not do so runs the risk of seeing old age itself as an illness that is inevitable and untreatable, with the attendant risk of rationing or unjustly depriving older people of modern and sophisticated treatments, simply on the basis of their age. The Macmillan Cancer Support organisation highlighted its concerns in a 2012 report about the growing body of evidence to suggest that older people with cancer in the United Kingdom are under-treated, particularly when it comes to the use of chemotherapy. However, many older patients have emerged from the other side of treatment. What lessons have those tough older birds who have come through the personal crisis that is cancer have to teach the rest of us?

The older we become, the more familiar we are with all kinds of health setbacks. As doctors, when we think of a person, they sometimes brings to mind a window that admits light and air and allows one to see in as well as out. What kind of systemic window do we find in an older person? After many years of life, there may be a few cracks and areas of cloudiness in the glass in the form of chronic illnesses and perhaps a reduction in vitality. Do we value antique glass more highly or do we discard it in favour of a fresher, more transparent equivalent? Remember, it may still function just as well as newer glass in terms of excluding draughts, rattling less and repelling wayward missiles. If we intervene with treatments for the 50 percent of people over 65 who have two or more chronic illnesses, does the window become more or less clouded? Do we do more harm than good when applying invasive treatments to serious illness in later life? How do we get the right balance for each person?

Age is the greatest risk factor for developing cancer. Sixty percent of people who have cancer are 65 or older, but so are 60 percent of cancer survivors. For years, specialists believed that cancer was less aggressive in older people, and for some types of cancers, especially breast and prostate cancer, this may be true. Cancer treatment, therefore, may not need to be as radical for some older patients. However, this is quite a general statement as it depends on the location of the tumour and the risk of complications. For the more philosophical and quirkier candidates of reconstructive surgery, there may be at least some consolation from the installation of new body parts if we end up with a new organ or a metal knee that is a lot sturdier than the original. Whether they come with a lifetime guarantee, however, is another matter entirely.

Cancer, no matter how it is dressed up, is not a welcome houseguest, but it doesn't have to be a death sentence either. Although at no stage in life can we control every situation and its outcome, we can control our attitudes and how we deal with those situations. No one smiles because they have just been diagnosed with cancer, although smiles may be part of the eventual journey. A positive attitude may not solve all or any of life's problems, but it will certainly puzzle and maybe even annoy some people to make it worth the effort!

The American actress Christina Applegate spoke of how humour helped her battle breast cancer as she 'laughed more in the hospital than ever before . . . making fun of all the weird things that were happening to me' whilst recovering from cancer surgery in the Cedars-Sinai Medical Centre in Los Angeles in 2008. Sometimes, all we can do when faced with our own mortality (a scenario not unfamiliar to the existentially inquisitive older person) is to laugh to keep ourselves from crying. We are entitled to whatever coping mechanism works for us to get us through the shock and trauma of cancer, be it tears or laughter. Fear is felt by many older people suffering with cancer: fear of what is coming next, fear of the treatment, fear of letting people down if the wish is to opt out of invasive or overly aggressive therapy. People should realise this fear is completely acceptable – it merely indicates how brave our intent is. No matter how bad things are, cancer can't invade the soul or steal eternal life, nor can it destroy friendship, suppress memories or silence courage. As people who have gone through chemotherapy frequently tell me, there is very little left in life that can really scare them. Some older people seem to stoically accept the pain and get on with life, difficult and all as it must be. It is as if they burn off the emotion that should logically threaten to overwhelm them as a fuel for their final journey.

As a practising clinician who works with older people who have developed mental-health difficulties as a reaction to cancer and other illnesses, I frequently admire their humour, such as the patient who groaned at the prospect of yet another MRI scan as it could cause her to stick to the fridge. I also recall a lady wearing a headscarf who boasted of paying her oncologist 'big bucks for this hairstyle' and who calculated that she would save money by not having to get her hair done.

Survival rates for most cancer types are steadily improving; having lived many years does not disqualify a person from looking for more. One of the triumphs of the twentieth century has been the improvement in our life expectancy. There is a 'can' in cancer, because as a society we *can* and are beating it. Having fought through the bad days of absorbing the diagnosis and the treatment, older people have earned better days, especially their place at the party on National Cancer Survivors Day.

Brexit (In)Dependence Day

On 23 June 2016 the electorate of Great Britain decided, for better or for worse, that their partnership of over 43 years with the European Union should end. As the dust continues to swirl in the fallout of this momentous decision, there has been an accusation that nostalgic elderly Brexiters (who apparently voted *en masse* for Britain to leave the European Union) have stolen the future of an entire younger generation, removing them from collaboration and cooperation with the union into which they were born. The narrative that an older segment of the electorate has deliberately stymied the idealism of fresh-faced, virginal voters is nothing new. The tabloid mantra of politics and political activity has long claimed that as older voters get more stuff, young people get stuffed. Older people are often accused of being more rigid, ideologically right-wing and conservative in their views as they age, and therefore vulnerable to the processes of ageing that tend to make people resistant to change.

Is this anything more than a subconscious and overly scrupulous reaction to the duties and perhaps burdens of middle age such as mating, marriage, mortgage and procreation? Does it stem from a desire to protect and insulate those endeavours, thereby clinging to the prevailing social order that preserves them, or do a range of crabby, crusty habits and attitudes inevitably harden as we grow older? The maxim variously attributed to Winston Churchill, Benjamin Disraeli and Victor Hugo that 'any man who is under 30 and is not a liberal has no heart and any man who is over 30 and is not a conservative has no brains' is not just an unintended insult to female suffragettes but may describe the psychological entrenchment that awaits the precocious utopia-seeker in later life.

There is little doubt that when it comes to the elections for positions of high political office (despite the resultant lows of politics such as corruption, cronyism and broken promises), older people still spend their votes like drunken sailors, whereas the young prudishly abstain. In the US midterm elections of November 2010, 61 percent of citizens aged 65 and older voted, in contrast to 21 percent of citizens aged 18 to 24 who bothered to cast a ballot, according to the US Census bureau. There is a concern that apathy and disillusionment underlie the waning youth vote and that this in turn is matched by the indifference of many political parties to the concerns of younger voters; to some extent these trends seem to feed off each other. Whilst younger generations are relaxed about using their votes, it should come as little surprise that older voters may map out more of the political agenda. Senior citizens are more likely to vote than younger people because retirees not only have valuable government benefits to protect but also because older voters don't move from abode to abode without putting down roots or registering to vote. Senior citizens also have more time to mull over all things political and to take a relaxed sojourn to their voting location. Just as young folk come under a certain peer pressure to rebel and be uncompromisingly idealistic, so older voters face a certain pressure to conform to social norms within their community and to turn out on election day, just like their friends and neighbours. It is not to say, however, that younger activists are entirely absent from the political process. Younger people are frequently the creators and instigators of major social change across the world, albeit often based on single issues such as the Vietnam War protests, the tragedy of Tiananmen Square in China or more recently the Black Lives Matter campaign in the US.

The electoral absenteeism of the youth demographic constitutes yet another reason for elders to engage in the popular pastime of denunciation of the young who have been relentlessly bashed in time-honoured fashion since humans could converse. As fewer young voters exercise their democratic franchise, there is no guarantee that they will ever invest, albeit as latecomers, in the national Ponzi scheme that is the democratic election. If younger members of society remain under a generational guardianship or virtual representation, how will the angry young Turks actually learn the skills necessary to harness and adapt established traditions and eventually rule over their country? It is also up to political parties to encourage participation of the youth in democratic processes, and when this is done effectively, the status quo can be challenged.

The younger generation may have a point, however, when it comes to the full utilisation of their franchise, in that if they are deemed old enough to fight and die for their country and even to vote out the government that compels them to do so, then are they not old enough to run for the highest office in the land? The age requirements that exist for the Federal Office in the United States, such as a bar on candidates aged less than 35 running for the presidency, can be seen as antiquated, imprudent and even as a pernicious form of state-sanctioned discrimination. If an intergenerational war is to be avoided, the body politic needs a new and inclusive model of social participation for all citizens, irrespective of age. The young may feel entitled to ask questions about the implications of demographic ageing for under-resourced and fragile economies, and older people may demand changes in social policy that see many talented individuals ejected from the workplace because they have reached 65 years of age. Above all, every political system requires legislators with enough foresight and vision to see beyond their own generational interests. Most common concerns span the divide between extremes of age in our society. It is notable that both older and younger generations are concerned with a range of similar issues such as tax rates, security, crime and medical and insurance matters.

Above all, older people must believe firmly in the positive contribution they have to make to the realm of politics, because of and not in spite of their age. In the United States, we're continuing to see a greying of the Senate (the average age of the 2014 elected body being 62) yet in relation to world politics, youth is the current flavour of the month, with a swathe of countries electing leaders in their 30s including Austria, New Zealand, France and Ireland. The essential message must be that no one should be excluded from full participation in politics on the grounds of age and in reality, older people are more likely to face discrimination in this context. Winston Churchill, a seasoned politician, observed an older MP struggling to hear a dreary speech from one of the less inspiring MPs by using an ear trumpet. He is claimed to have inquired about the identity of the older MP in the midst of this particularly dull contribution: 'Who is that fool denying his natural advantages?' The diminution of some sensory inputs with age can therefore occasionally be merciful and even advantageous for some political careers.

Father's Day for Grandpas

Father's Day is a special day dedicated to honouring fathers and father-hood, which in many countries is held on the third Sunday in June. Whilst younger fathers may have become accustomed to receiving breakfast in bed (as their wives or partners do on Mother's Day) and an occasional pair of socks or an electronic gadget, should older fathers and grandfathers expect the royal treatment on this day, or in reality has the memory of all their past contributions to family life been swept away like the crumbs from all that bread they put on the table over the years?

Grandparenthood is perhaps the ideal state of human nurturing, whereby love and affection can be poured out in abundance, but then those tender objects of affection can be sent home without the respon-sibility of launching them into wider society as trusty, accomplished, tax-paying adults. Compared to grandmothers, grandfathers anecdo-tally may tend to take up more of the backseat of life when it comes to assisting their own offspring with childminding chores. There are other priorities in life after all, such as warming barstools, doing DIY chores at a snail's pace or tapping little white balls into holes in the ground. Whether the next generation of grandparents will stick to such outdated gender roles is another matter entirely. It would be reasonable to assume that a longevity dividend would apply to older men who have such an idyllic existence, but in a cruelly ironic twist, nature instead dictates that the more productive and useful members of society, namely grandmothers, are the ones who enjoy, on average, a six-year survival advantage over their male counterparts. The moral of the story of later life thus remains that contribution always wins out over inertia, even for those who may have worn themselves out from work during their lifetimes and who crave the footstool of stagnation in retirement. Can the occasion of Father's Day be useful to rekindle the role of men in family life or is it simply another retail-driven opportunity to stuff older men's caves with even more gadgets and gizmos?

The reality for many older dads and granddads is that when it comes to honouring their paternal contribution to family life, a gift becomes the main focus for the day. Most of us have already exercised the gatherer part of the hunter-gatherer instinct to excess and have more than enough objects on their shelves, thank you very much. As ever, sensible gift-giving ground rules emphasise gifts that reflect the tastes, interests and hobbies of the person involved. Older men who are active may have completely different preferences compared to those who are less active by choice or because of illness and mobility restriction. It may be sensible to give consumable gifts that older people can immediately use and enjoy, but it may be equally quite tactless to imply that the recipient is so chronologically deprived that they are merely waiting at the departure gates for the final boarding call. Consumable gifts do not just include treats between meals but can be a ticket to an event, a subscription to a magazine or even a voucher for a service such as the thoughtful payment for the rental of a golf buggy for a whole year. If the donor can afford to add two or three years to this facility, the flattery implicit in the expected length of the recipient's survival in order to get the full benefit from this gift will be of inestimable value. Although age-appropriate gifts are logical, they must not be patronising, nor should they dwell on any disability stereotypes of later life. The offspring of an older person need not be surprised, therefore, by exhortations to take back an inappropriate gift such as a childish jigsaw puzzle from the gaze of the older recipient on Father's Day.

A hobby-related gift or token of appreciation is ideal on Father's Day. What better way to exercise a real largesse than to offer the most precious resource of your time as the metaphorical wrapping paper for the said offering? For example, testing out a new fishing rod over the weekend can make for much bonding and reminiscing; however, unpacking historical baggage from earlier family life that results in loud arguments may scare the fish away and should be avoided at all costs. Of course, a gift that implies an investment of personal time and effort by the donor may be most appreciated, such as a meal before the latest operatic or symphonic reconstruction. A personalised gift of a music CD or a bestselling book may be received with great joy if it aligns with any meticulously dropped hints before Father's Day. The temptation of the younger generation to drag Granddad into the digital era by purchasing a Kindle to store the remaining 9,999 Father's Day tomes should be seriously questioned, however, unless the benefactor intends to follow up this gift with endless hours of live demonstration time. The path to progress is indeed paved with good inventions as well as multiple frustrations, as any older parent who has had to give driving lessons to their offspring will attest.

It is obvious that Father's Day for older dads and granddads is about more than the material gift, particularly if the whole occasion has slipped the mind of one's offspring! Never short of ways to spare the blushes of those youthful multi-taskers, it may be up to a wily senior to hint at substitute gifts-in-kind such as the helping out with the day's chores. Assistance with transport, an offer of a haircut or a scenic drive will more than provide for the great providers in one's life.

July

Happy Days

Just as the memory of the winter blues has finally dispersed and the slate-grey sky is warmed by the heat of the mid-summer sun, a day arrives which, according to our Blue Monday guru Dr Cliff Arnall, has been mathematically proven to be the happiest day of the year. Having carried out research for Walls, the ice-cream brand, and claiming no ethical conflict of interest, celebrity psychologist Dr Arnall devised a mathematical 'happiness formula' whose equation used numbers to represent positivity factors including social interaction, weather, nature, holiday anticipation and memories of childhood summers. So far, the date for Arnall's happiest day of the year has varied, falling close to Midsummer in the Northern Hemisphere (June the 21 to the 24) in previous years but in 2017, according to the formula, July 14 was set as maximum happiness day. In fairness to Dr Arnall (who has been unable to feel happiness on any day since his work has been slated as pseudo-scientific by his fellow academics), he has claimed the main aim of his research is to get people talking about what makes them happy. Does the fact that the hard science behind the 'Happiest Day' has melted away like the proverbial ice cream in the sun mean we should ignore total strangers telling us to be happy? Do we purr, cat-like, as we get the said (ice) cream, or would we do well to inhale life's laughing gas and reflect on the true elements of happiness? After all, the happiest day of the year may be viewed as a distinct improvement on the most depressing one. Can older people expect their happiness reserves to plummet with each advancing year, or are the golden years true to their name, with 24-carat contentment rather than a superficial plating of happiness?

To the young and perhaps naive, any happiness for elders that is still accessible in later life seems rather thin. The rock star Pete Town-shend admitted in a 2012 *Guardian* interview that he had remarked 50 years earlier that 'oldies looked awfully cold' and that he wrote lyrics but never sang about how he hoped to die before he reached old age. Although no subsequent quotes on the subject of old age are recorded or attributed to the guitarist, he may have worried about a shortage in supplies of LSD in future years and the inevitable popping of his happy party balloon. There is much genuine confusion about which day is the happiest day of the year. Should it be the first payday after Blue Monday, when the deposit on the summer holiday/reality-escape has been paid, or perhaps New Year's Eve, or Christmas Day itself? Then there is Thanksgiving Day for Americans, the start of daylight saving time in March, or the UN-sponsored International Day of Happiness on the 20 of March. The entire month of August has also been denoted as a period of time when optimal happiness may exist, as the foot is taken off life's accelerator during annual holidays. In actual fact, the choice for the happiest day of the year is as arbitrary as the whimsical selection of toppings on one of those Walls ice creams.

It was the Dalai Lama who said that happiness is a quest that keeps us going, but it also keeps going in our endless scramble for euphoria, excitement and distraction. As the view of the life ahead closes in as we age, one could argue that older people are more in touch with uncomfortable realities than heedless youngsters and backward glances at missed opportunities and regrets are inevitable. There is embedded in these assumptions, however, that younger people are simply magicked into this world with boundless confidence and beauty, into lives devoid of struggle. In reality, no stage of life is without its scuffles – take late adolescence with all the hidden insecurities of trying to establish an identity that doesn't involve painful piercings or fitting into a peer group that aspires to come first in the shop-lifters league table. What about the perturbation of striving to placate others, be they the boss, bank manager or future joint signatory on the mortgage application? Midlife can offer a steady diet of hassles for the so-called sandwich generation, where they can feel like they are perpetually filling in the middle of the sandwich as they try to provide for dependent children and ageing parents. While sandwiches and their unfortunate middle layers may figuratively be in abundance, picnics are few and far between for those between youth and old age, who are squeezed by pressures from above and demands from below.

One of the more refreshing aspects of ageing, and perhaps the best way of defying any age-related decline, is the reclaiming (or experiencing for the first time) of a carefree spirit and the letting go of the hidden anxieties that did so much dirty work in the past. Nothing is so inherently and invincibly 'young' as our true selves freed from worries about money, relationships or the different kinds of success that we may have been obsessed with in our forties and fifties. The fires kindled by burning ambition may not have consumed us, but they probably did kill off the undergrowth of our happiness in our earlier years. Because our years ahead are fewer than those behind, we can finally accept things, prioritise and see the wood from the trees. In many ways, those individuals who appear to be most content seem to live most firmly in the present and neither look forward with too much trepidation nor backwards with too much regret. They have enough emotional capacity to manage threats to happiness that come from unexpected losses or adversity. Although it can be tempting to hang our expectations for happiness on a single, special or nominated day, the challenge is to make the other 364 days of the year as meaningful as possible.

The notion of the happiest day of the year and the harmless bemusement it induces has no upper age limit – after all, laughter, like eating those Walls ice creams, doesn't require teeth or expensive implants!

Disobedience Day – Live a Little at Last

International Disobedience Day is celebrated on the 3 July each year. The origin is somewhat unclear as the originators clearly disobeyed calls to accurately record their motives and identity, but theories exist to support the view that it was established to promote the benefits of civil disobedience. The current crop of seniors amongst us have more than a sneaking regard for acts of historical civil disobedience, as rebellion against twentieth-century tyrants frequently meant obedience to the higher power of God. Of course, interest in one's maker and how they may be placated usually becomes a prime preoccupation for those about to pass through the pearly gates; being a martyr for a good cause also looks great on one's CV. Perhaps Disobedience Day was created by people who had no greater vision in mind other than to express frustration at having spent their entire lives doing what someone else told them to. While Robert E. Lee, the Confederate Civil War general, once famously said that 'obedience to lawful authority is the foundation of manly character', a century and a half later, discerning and moral disobedience frequently replaces blind compliance as the new civic virtue of our times. If obedience occurs when a person is told to do something, and conformity happens through social pressure (the norms of the majority), have older people earned the right to be selective in the deference they pay toward such rules of society, or is this a slippery slope toward the disintegration of community and civilization?

In my experience, older people generally like to present themselves as biddable, even supplicant, and often confer an ill-deserved respect upon figures of authority. This stereotype isn't universally true for all elders, however, with the feisty ones being unable to resist infringing since they first pilfered sweets as an urchin. Guilt may be a great inhibitor in terms of being tempted by transgressions and is to the spirit what physical pain is to the body, but if we were aware of all the cash we could save by refusing fines for minor offences and going to prison instead, perhaps we would tear up those parking tickets, shoplift and divest ourselves of clothing in public. This could ensure we would be fed, housed and entertained in centrally heated quarters with no bills to pay. The attraction of being able to get your teeth fixed and other health check-ups in prison may threaten to engulf the entire penal system with a senior snarl up. In countries like Korea and Japan, where the populations are sizably-aged, senior citizens are committing petty crimes in bigger numbers than teenagers. Japanese government statistics revealed in 2011 that the number of people aged 65 and over charged with a criminal offence rose six-fold over the previous two decades. Poverty, loneliness and boredom may be factors in creating mini gangster-grannies, but some veteran older male offenders see themselves as quasi-businessmen who maintain lifelong criminal connections. Because of their greying locks, they may pass under the radar and continue their misdemeanours, thereby avoiding the eventual lock-up. In a vault-heist in England in 2015, however, the seven criminals who were apprehended weren't so lucky. They ranged in age from 43 to 76, with a combined age of 432. The UK's *Daily Mail* described the group as 'looking more like ageing golfing buddies than a sophisticated criminal gang'. While some notorious older villains have stained the pages of history, not everyone who disobeys societal norms to the extent of acquiring a criminal record is a criminal psychopath of the grey variety.

Disobedience may be a useful way in which older people reject society's edicts to disengage and become passive and submissive. Being outrageous is an exaggeration of a positive stereotype of older people that sees non-conformity as a way of communicating a new identity. Outrageous behaviour allows the fullest expression of previously suppressed impulses, yet if this personality change is too rapid, a brain disorder such as dementia is likely to be queried and the person could find themselves under an MRI scanner quicker than the punchline of a bad joke. While this is undoubtedly prompted by concern for the owner of that ageing cerebral cortex, family members may be looking for reassurance that their loved one is not about to disperse their inheritance to worthy causes such as animal sanctuaries or deprived golfers. Jenny Joseph's poem 'Warning' (1961) contains a defiant declaration against the narrow strictures of propriety and convention, as the writer states that she will 'pick flowers in other people's gardens [...] learn to spit' and do many more outlandish things to 'make up for the sobriety of my youth'. Souping up one's mobility scooter, drugs, daredevil sports and promiscuity are but a few legal and illegal ways to let down what is left of one's hair.

Disobedience may in fact be a way of refuelling the mind to sustain one's independence, which comes under threat in a myriad of ways as we age. If older people are to engage in socially acceptable acts of defiance and thumb their collective noses at censoriousness and disapproval, a pretence of deafness, mild confusion and ignorance of prevailing rules can double the mischievous value of their gestures. Someone who is beyond the reach of the tut-tutting of the many sanctimonious teachers, advisers and consultants who have set themselves up to manage our lives can be a champion of the free spirit. Older people can thereby attain bragging rights amongst an entire generation who seek revenge for a life weighted with pressure to succeed and whose natural abilities were suffocated by obedience and conformity.

Thankfully, blind obedience in our present times is not only in short supply but is something of a dirty word. Canines rather than humans get sent to obedience school these days. Even older fathers can rarely expect automatic obedience (except on Father's Day when they urge their offspring not to spend a lot of money on their gift and are offended when the same progeny meekly comply). As a society, we now know that doing something just because it is perceived to be good is not a sufficient reason for doing it. Older people know that disobedience can be the dark side of free will and may have very little to lose as they see through exhortations to comply. In an era of soft power, where absolute edicts are unpopular, yet subtle thought-control through advertising and media reigns supreme, a degree of individually expressed anarchy on Disobedience Day is surely called for.

Nelson Mandela Day

Nelson Mandela Day was inaugurated on 18 July 2009 in recognition of the elder statesman's birthday. In honouring his life's work, there is also an implicit call for people to take action to change the world for the better. Far from being a parochial excuse for a South-African-led siesta, Nelson Mandela Day is a global notable when it comes to inspiring citizens of the planet to scrutinise injustice, deprivation and waste and to take small actions to remedy such matters. I frequently refer to Nelson Mandela as a role model for older people in one of my regular patient lectures at St. Patrick's Hospital. Here is a man who effectively began as opposed to ended his political career in his 70s and whose release from prison heralded the transformation of an entire nation. Far from retiring into the background to write memoirs or lecture to the world about injustice, Mandela the pensioner and former prisoner rolled up his sleeves and set about mapping out the post-apartheid, non-violent, democratic journey for his people through a unique combination of charm, wisdom and determination. Mandela was the master reconciler as he embraced the culture and language of his former jailers, studying the psyche and mentality of the white prison staff on Robben Island, and even learning Afrikaans. These were skills that allowed him to understand and subsequently negotiate with the former architects of apartheid.

The example Nelson Mandela set, whose personal sacrifice in pursuit of the freedom of his people was commendable, is undoubtedly inspiring when it comes to beginning a hoped-for ripple of good deeds throughout the world. Any objective historian will recall, however, that it wasn't always thus with Madiba, as he moved from endorsing armed resistance to the apartheid regime as a young leader to being one of the most important leaders of the ANC during his prolonged period of political and personal isolation throughout his long incarceration. We should ask ourselves thus if ageing and the accompanying mellowing process has a major role in transforming a person from an agitator to a placid peacemaker and model elder statesman?

Most systems of governance have one thing in common: the serial selection of older men and women for positions of global leadership. Whether it is the position of United Nations Secretary General or even long-standing dictator, eminent, senior members of society are frequently selected to cast a wise eye over the prevailing political landscape and to issue stern edicts whenever a status quo is threatened. For example, when the students of Tiananmen Square protested for democracy and caught the leadership of the Chinese Communist Party off guard in 1989, it was the party elders who resolved to use force to suppress the fledgling democratic movement. These ideological dinosaurs didn't have to take crash courses in tank driving or brandishing pistols themselves, however. Their bile, combined with the brawn of younger soldiers who were brought into Beijing to do the killing, was a deadly mix in snuffing out any hopes for political reform behind the Great Wall.

Those erudite folk in possession of grey locks (or wisdom highlights as they may be euphemistically reframed) and in positions of responsibility within the body politic such as a ceremonial president or elder statesman or woman may offer low-key, unofficial advice as to its continued well-being; by and large, this is well-intentioned and benevolent. The arena of day-to-day politics and public discourse today is too often frenetic, divisive and reactive, even when appearances suggest that all is allegedly well with democratic institutions. The divisiveness of the 2016 US presidential election is a case in point. Many feel that contemporary politics focuses too much on style as opposed to substance or policy, leading to political alienation and electoral cynicism. The presence of elder statesmen and women in advisory roles provides a contemplative and necessary detachment, as well as time needed for clarity and calm, which all kinds of crisis demand from time to time. The recent reminders of the value of Northern Ireland's 1998 Good Friday Agreement by its original authors, who perceived threats to its continued existence, was prescient in the light of Brexit. It was Cicero who stated that the great affairs of life are not performed by physical strength, activity or nimbleness of body but by character and expression of opinion. Those of an old age possess these to a great degree. Statesmanship in the embodiment of Nelson Mandela conveys a quality of leadership that organically brings people together, irrespective of nationality or creed. Central to this idea is a spirit of caring for others, and this attribute is one that has a global appeal. Older leaders may have a role in peace-making, dispute-prevention and adjudication, despite waning energies precluding them from making love or war. Those firebrands in many countries around the world who initially terrorised and traumatised may eventually reincarnate into peaceful protagonists with the mantle of leadership, the assumption of responsibility for others and plain old conflict fatigue. Prison rations for most become even less digestible with age, and the appeal of alternative ways to gently shake the world and inspire others to do similarly becomes stronger. Such a transformation will not only be a great career move for would-be statesmen and women, but can also aid their causes, which may be landlocked into cul-de-sacs. Only a wise, old head may see this and proportion their remaining beliefs in any enterprise or cause because of its continued relevance. Persuasion by an older standard-bearer can also help younger hotheads and radicals cool their heels by abandoning conflict or deciding to enter negotiations. An older dove with a lengthy flying mileage on the clock is arguably better placed than a young hawk to effect strategic change within a movement. Older statesmen and women who last the political pace and who are untarnished by corruption and cronyism can come to embody the core values of any struggle – Mahatma Gandhi of India and Emmeline Pankhurst of Britain's Suffragettes being notable examples. Revered elders may also be intolerant of political trendiness as they slap down the dilution of core principles or what they perceive to be juvenile political heresy. Perhaps a minority of elder statesmen and women will always prefer to remain Castro-like, at the centre, rather than at the edge of power.

As mentioned, Nelson Mandela has been a role model for older people who hope to influence others. Whilst his initial incarceration was brutalising, it also allowed for the incubation of his political ideals, which came to fruition during his presidency, from 1994 to 1999. This shows that not only do good things come to those who wait, but good things happen to those who develop and grow into the most temperate, balanced and erudite version of themselves. On 18 July, by devoting 67 minutes, or one minute for every year of Mandela's public service, to helping others, people of all ages can make a small gesture of solidarity and a step toward a global movement for good.

Birthday Child

As the weeks slide by, there is one week that stands out in our consciousness: the week surrounding our birthday, when we may feel entitled to every wish and our family and friends are expected to bow to our whims of fancy. As the birthday diva matures, however, and the only gift that may be sought is to be no longer reminded of the annual celebration of one's life, is the inner child still ageless? Does it demand more cake, extra attention and other material reminders that we are loved and important to those around us? Are the best birthdays those that have yet to arrive or should we simply embrace the inevitable without apology or explanation?

When we were young, 24 hours seemed a grossly inadequate period of time in which to celebrate our birth or announce our higher status to the world, such as the arrival of our sixteenth or twenty-first year. Receiving everything we wished for or doing outrageous deeds almost compelled the need for a longer time period in which to celebrate our personal festivities. Like a sixteenth-century monarch with a strong narcissistic streak, the platform of the birthday meant a youngster could spin out the celebration for a weekend or even a week, not counting the anticipation and preparation necessary for the party of the year. Not all cultures or religious denominations are apparently so self-obsessed, however. The Jehovah's Witnesses declare that they do not celebrate birthdays. Even those who earnestly embrace a seemingly flat-line existence through tight religious stricture must acknowledge that perhaps the greatest annual feast in our social calendar (Christmas) is a prolonged birthday bash with multiple trimmings.

Once over the proverbial hill of life or at least half-way up, a subtle and creeping ambivalence spreads about the subject of advancing and compulsory chronology and how, or if at all, it should be acknowledged. At one level it could be argued that birthdays are good for one's health as statistics show that people who have the most live the longest, yet, being reminded of our mortality compels many to slip into something more comfortable (such as denial) as we grow in years. It may be socially diplomatic to remember the birthday of a loved one and simultaneously forget their age. Sending a generic birthday card without the raw number crudely etched onto the cardboard or the detachable plastic badge may be seen as appropriately sensitive. The human mind has apparently endless capacities for denial in that, irrespective of our score, we often personally define old age as being five to ten years older than we are! Nonetheless, many eventually reach a point when they stop lying about their age and actually start bragging about it. After all, the only way to have a long and happy life is to accumulate birthdays.

If we are to party the night (or the afternoon) away and pay more than just a respectful nod to those ageing milestones, there are some solid ground-rules to observe that can ensure the overall success of the event. Depending on the physical well-being of the birthday boy or girl, we should plan assistance with transport and mobility, not only for ourselves but also for friends, associates and other partners in crime. The best-laid plans of mice and men often crumble like birthday cake in the face of illness or other calamities, so having postponement arrangements at the ready in the face of temporary but necessary unavailability would be prudent. A full risk-assessment and analysis of all conceivable dangers may be called for, ranging in scope from awareness of the weather forecast on the big day to detailed knowledge of the venue, including wheelchair accessibility, toilets and fire exits. Arranging for oxygen cylinders to be on standby may be unnecessarily fatalistic and is potentially insulting to your birthday guests, whose presence we celebrate in expectation of many future birthdays during the years ahead. Equating old age with illness is, after all, highly stigmatising and can stifle the inner fourteen-year-old child trying to emerge from the eighty-year-old body during the birthday frivolities.

Remembering to include preferences and personal interests of the birthday beneficiary is also crucial for any birthday event. This also shifts the focus tactfully away from the rawness of one's birthday age being celebrated and gives the organisers a chance to be creative when designing themes for the party of the year. Deciding on the party venue, menu, allergy list (including reactions to unwanted guests) and the roll-call of desired invitees is essential. Party decorations include personal makeovers. Spending a week polishing the house misses the point entirely about who or what is going to be the centre of attention on the big day. In a crowded room, people are more likely to lavish attention on you, the birthday honouree, rather than notice how neatly the cushions line up. Pre-sunset start times may betray a certain physical squeamishness and frailty; whilst early start times are perfectly acceptable in a sedate tea party in a nursing home, they should be avoided if one doesn't want to party old. An eagerness to tidy up too promptly, even before the party really gets going, should be resisted as guests may question their investment of time and effort in attending. They may feel like retracting all those compliments during toasting if the dreaded black-plastic sack appears too early, hinting at a desire by the host for an early exodus. Bright lights and cheap booze must also feature on the banned list, as every wrinkle will have been surely noticed before the unpalatable booze eventually dulls powers of observation. Anyone who wishes to create a photo album of the birthday event should be aware that having the shoes to match the bags under one's eyes does not console those wishing to conceal age-revealing blemishes. It is socially considerate to be discreet about the camera lens and not brandish it like a highwayman's pistol in these circumstances. A written souvenir book of signatures and messages to be filled in by the guests may be more discreet and gain greater participation from guests than a camera that refuses to lie.

However you choose to party, a wealth of clichés is available to comfort the longevity shy – most of which are to be found on birthday cards. My own favourite is 'the more candles on your cake, the hotter you are'. Only don't burn your fingers lighting them.

AUGUST

Chill Out in August

During summertime's easy living, practicing the art of relaxation and escaping from modern living looms large in the minds of many who flock to places far and near in an attempt to find that perfect sanctuary. While the young and middle-aged are prone to suffering from high-stress and high-velocity lifestyles and have good reason to remove the foot from life's speed pedals, what about the older generation? They are less likely to be so firmly handcuffed to the sources of stress such as work, family commitments and financial pressure.

For some older people, relaxation may be somewhat threatening to a momentum they have built in earlier times when they moved through life at a certain speed in order to be busy, useful, free of guilt and indispensable to others. This rush may be very difficult to step away from; by sticking to these old habits we can also avoid unpleasant feelings, thoughts and questions such as what we are feeling, longing for, and lacking in our lives. Sterling Moss, the former Formula One racing driver, epitomised a flamboyant, danger-loving addiction to the fast lane of life and once said 'It's necessary to relax your muscles when you can but relaxing your brain is fatal'. Moss indirectly implied that if you double the pace at which you live, you can live twice as much as your nearest life rival/racing competitor. There is also the implication that declining distraction can turn you into an isolated recluse, leaving the way open for the rot of mental decrepitude. The summer season may force a period of solitude on an older person, however, as family and neighbours go on holiday, leaving the individual isolated with little variation in their day and little to look forward to. Existential questions may haunt during these moments of remoteness unless we can take a step back and use alternative strategies such as learning one of the many forms of active relaxation including gentle breathing exercises or movement-based meditative practices such as yoga. A decline in energy, fragmented sleep and the limitations of movement that some older people experience necessarily implies that they can't pack as much activity into their schedules. Therefore, they must look at alternatives to the hectic pace and extreme levels of stimulation that they once experienced.

Active relaxation may seem indulgent, unnecessary and the preserve of refugees from the flower-power era, but it is truly a vital life skill. Smart employers who want to boost the productivity of their workers have seized on mindfulness classes for their stressed and potentially underperforming employees. It may best be defined as a broader form of letting go and includes practices that have been part of Eastern traditions for thousands of years. These practices include meditation and mindfulness – the art of paying attention. Older people may be better placed to embrace active relaxation and practice these skills of calming one's mind and thereby opening one's heart. Younger folk who are ensnared by the technological modernity of today's digital world may have greater difficulty avoiding distraction. Older people realise, through life experience and accumulated wisdom, that far from needing to rush to a distant beach at the point of burnout and mental clutter, a permanent state of mind that appreciates the marvels that lie hidden in everyday life is more likely to sustain our interest, energy and enthusiasm. The perfect escape or golden retreat may be less about buying entertainment and more about creating our own simple pleasures, observing them clearly and noticing the rich texture and details of the world around us. This is not about sluggishness, laziness or disengagement from the world around us. It is about fully connecting with our external reality, one which is mediated by calmness and clarity. As a result of skilful detachment, the world will come to nourish those who practice it. Through regular use of relaxation techniques, older people can come to a place of calmness, self-awareness, open-heartedness, be able to face challenges and be present. Yoga, t'ai chi and mindfulness are some of the meditative disciplines that older people are flocking to. They have become mainstream practices, even in the psychiatric in-patient campus where I work.

No matter how short or long our remaining time on this earth is, we can build a better, healthier and more fulfilling relationship with that time by incorporating a larger perspective into our everyday lives. This means we may be able to face the bigger questions such as our mortality, our priorities, and the removal of obstacles that prevent us from doing the things we want to. Our thoughts may turn to what we want to contribute to the time that comes after ours. Building a legacy is something we do all the time, and consciously reflecting on this is neither vain nor self-indulgent, but a supremely mindful and creative act. Carving out the time required to enter into peaceful, mindful relaxation may require cunning and strategy (such as avoiding onerous babysitting duties during the summer months). Managing the expectations of one's offspring may be crucial to avail of opportunities to empty the mind and truly focus on the present moment. If this relaxed state results in a slackening of the rules that govern being older, the younger generation will eventually thank you for this legacy.

International Forgiveness Day

International Forgiveness Day takes place on the first Sunday in August each year. Forgiveness has been defined as an intentional act and voluntary process whereby a person who feels they have been wronged undergoes a change in feelings toward the offender. It is about letting go of negative emotions such as vengefulness, and difficult as it may seem, wishing the offender well. For older people, the opportunity to stew in the juice of past conflicts and grudges can seem irresistible. Although the number of accumulated enemies seems to verify that one actually lived a life in the first place, there comes a realisation that disputes are rarely black and white and that to make mistakes, even wilfully, is part of being human. Conversely, applying the socially laudable version of the 'F word', namely 'Forgiveness', is potentially divine, as Oscar Wilde said. It was also Oscar Wilde who advised forgiveness of one's enemies because it was guaranteed to annoy them, perversely implying that forgiveness may be the greatest form of revenge! As the twilight of life beckons, what are the obstacles to healing old wounds rather than settling old scores?

As a clinician practising in geriatric mental health, I have too often witnessed conflicts, frequently intra-familial, that weigh older people down as they are frequently laced with long-standing bitterness and frozen hostility. These conflicts often become entwined with a range of mental-health difficulties for the person bearing the hurt. It reminds me of a suppurating wound that refuses to heal without radical excision. I often wonder if a good old 'air-clearing' verbal altercation would be the non-surgical equivalent of cleaning an infected laceration – a spectacle that is painful at the time but allows for better healing in the long-term. It is amazing how, after the storm of an argument has passed, close relationships can resume without any reference to the lengthy pause of many years. The policy of dispelling emotional tension through force of verbiage may be decidedly risky, however, if either party is prone to physical violence. Remember, walking sticks should only be employed as mobility aids and are not intended as weapons to destroy the opponent's motility. Sometimes, what remains unsaid is easiest to mend as a strong emotion such as anger is liable to render even the most astute, self-regulating senior a shade less restrained. Therefore, the policy of frank discussion to resolve disputes should not showcase sentiments that make matters worse as they can't be retracted. Nonetheless, for the older person in a hurry who wishes to have one last go at resolving antagonism, these pitfalls should not deter a noble attempt to apply the healing balm of forgiveness. Sometimes the first step in this regard may even be to understand that the other person is a complete idiot who deserves pity rather than contempt. A thorough filtering of this judgement would nevertheless be expedient in the interests of harmony and forgiveness.

It is often the case that once a person has issued forgiveness as a main course, the sins of the other get frequently reheated for breakfast; this should be resisted at all costs. Older adults should see fence-mending as the last-chance saloon, with ejection from the said premises of life being imminent. Hence, ambivalent or conditional forgiveness may be seen as a mean-spirited attempt to win an argument on only one set of terms. Often forgiveness is mistaken for weakness – in reality, forgiveness is not about condoning the perpetrator's behaviour or justifying the offence due to extenuating circumstances. Neither is forgiveness connected to the opportune forgetting or denial of the harmful impact of the perpetrator's behaviour. If two people do reconcile it is not because they have forgotten or entered a mutually convenient amnestic pact; rather, the forgiveness is both genuine and inherently generous. The act of forgiveness is different to reconciliation, however, and may not imply the rebuilding of an ongoing relationship with the perpetrator. For some, the prospect of being in the same room as the alleged malefactor is a severe stretch, never mind shacking up with them again.

What are the benefits of magnanimity of spirit for the older person, and how might they get there? We must first acknowledge the reluctance of some seniors to fully lower their guard and engage with the acts of (or the mindset of) gracious forgiveness. There exists a widely accepted life rule that to experience the same bite twice from an adversary implies a lack of caution and a deficit in common sense. Whilst older people may eventually welcome the changing perspectives that forgiveness brings to any life situation, they may be reluctant to forget lest they forgo the life lesson in the process; this may dilute the impact of forgiveness if it becomes half-hearted. Perhaps if absolution exists on a spectrum, some of it may be better than none, particularly if the forgiving donor wishes to benefit from forgiving and enjoy a reduction in depressive symptoms or the negative cardiovascular effects of chronic anger. Elevated blood pressure and an increased risk of heart disease are just some of the ways a simmering sense of anger can inflict a double hurt on those who deny forgiveness to others.

Exercises to boost forgiveness and lighten the weight of our hurt can include writing a letter to the person from the past that does not have to be sent, but which can release negativity and pain as we cathartically chart the wrongdoing and the associated emotions relating to the transgression. In case anyone forgets that they have forgiven and forgotten, forgotten how stupid they were to have been so upset in the first place or forgotten the existence of their erstwhile transgressor, a journaling session about the benefits of exercising past acts of forgiveness can be a useful resource to dip into as we strengthen our forgiveness muscles. This will also increase our self-awareness, allow us to reflect on our accrued wisdom and become a tad less sensitive in the process. For older people who wish to tidy up some of life's messes, forgiveness can be a vital piece of emotional decluttering to be undertaken before we in turn ask for forgiveness for ourselves from whoever we conceive our God to be and from those who would remember us and our example on that first Sunday in August.

Carry On Soaring

National Aviation Day is observed in the United States on August 19 each year to celebrate the history and development of the aviation industry. The day coincides with the birthday of Orville Wright, who along with his brother Wilbur invented and flew the first aircraft with controls on 17 December 1903 in Kitty Hawk, North Carolina. Aviation Day was established by Franklin D. Roosevelt and has endured well beyond twelve seconds, which was the duration of that first foray into the skies by the Wright brothers. Although the first flight covered only 120 feet, at that moment the past and the future of humanity seemed to separate, and the world began to shrink. The first scheduled commercial airline flight was conducted on January 1, 1914 by Tony Jannus. His airplane flew a distance of approximately 25 miles, with each passenger paying a $5 fare. The technological advances in aviation in just a few short decades have been nothing short of awe-inspiring since that first grainy photo of the Wright brothers' flying machine. Aircrafts have travelled into space, delivered weapons of mass destruction in wartime, assisted in communication and the mass movement of people. The aviation business has opened up global markets, radically changing trade and commercial activity as well as inspiring whole industries, including tourism. Whilst many older people have accumulated more than their share of air miles, should it be a case of airport desist rather than airport assist for seniors so that they can avoid the trials, tribulations and turbulence of flying?

Being able to travel safely and independently is highly prized by many older people. As doctors, we are frequently asked for advice about the medical risks of flying, and I recall one lady with a particularly challenging, fluctuating dementia and distressing visual hallucinations asking me about the feasibility of travelling alone to Zimbabwe to visit her son. My policy in this area is frequently to encourage the pursuit of travel as the confidence boost associated with a successful trip can last for many months. It may propel the person to experiment with and pursue other activities and challenges on their return. On this occasion, however, I discouraged this journey, fearing significant disorientation and agitation for the lady; I was reassured that the subject of my concern and her daughter fully understood and accepted my advice. A few weeks later, I received a postcard in an envelope from my patient, along with a photo of her and her safari guide in the back of a jeep in a Southern African game reserve. The trip had gone off without a hitch. We not only shared a laugh about this later, but my patient even encouraged me to show her holiday snaps to other risk-averse older travellers as proof of the benefits of taking a chance. Perhaps I shouldn't have worried so, as more airlines seem to focus now on 'hospital' rather than hospitality and carry more medical and resuscitation equipment than heretofore.

The health risks associated with air travel such as dehydration and immobilization leading to leg clots and deep vein thrombosis have been well publicised in recent years. Health hazards could be said to arise from the get-go, however, as older travellers can find the initial navigation of an airport to be downright disorientating. Risks of injury from being inadvertently pushed, shoved or tripped up from a suitcase falling from an overhead bin also needs to be considered. How those heavy, battering ram-like drinks trolleys don't crush more toes in the aisles I'll never know. That's not to mention the risk of exacerbating breathing problems or having a panic attack mid-flight due to the high altitude and low oxygen levels; all of these factors could cause one to seriously question the urge to go blasting through the skies in a pressurised metal tube or even to cancel the application for membership of the mile-high club. Harder to measure are the ill-effects of sharing bugs and microorganisms with fellow passengers in the one form of recycling that no one wishes to partake in: reconditioned air. While it may be less to do with the germ-laden air and more to do with the close proximity of bug-bearing fellow travellers, fumes and toxins of the engines from which the cabin air is drawn are said to pose a possible health risk to frequent flyers and cabin crew. Taxing the immune system as a result of fatigue, jet jag, sleep deprivation and the stress associated with flying may also make an older person more vulnerable to becoming sick. Perhaps the biggest health risk for senior flyers is the disruption to medication schedules due to jet lag and the crossing of different time zones. Do you take morning medication that is due upon night-time arrival or wait until the next day? This is no trivial matter if the medicine in question is vital; advice from your local pharmacist or family doctor in advance of making the trip can be helpful.

In my experience, the risks of air travel can be greatly mitigated by a few simple ground rules, the simplest and most important of which is to carry all one's medication in one's hand baggage rather than checking it into the hold with the rest of the kitchen sink. Although some people are reluctant to go through customs and security with tablets in tow in case they are treated like a drug mule, this is easily resolved by keeping medicines in their packaging and having a copy of your prescription. Having to answer questions in customs is infinitely better than being separated from one's precious medicines at your destination if the main luggage is erroneously sent to the furthest corner of the globe. Having adequate travel insurance is essential to traveling with peace of mind. Bear in mind, however, that some insurers blatantly discriminate against older people, especially if you have a pre-existing medical condition. Scrupulously examining the fine print with a magnifier is vital to uncovering those hidden restrictions. Keeping free alcoholic beverages to a minimum and resisting temptation is important as the diuretic effect of alcohol will only compound dehydration and jet lag; one should stay strong and minimally imbibe or abstain if you have taken a hypnotic or prescribed anti-anxiety tablet. Moving around the cabin is important to keep the circulation in good shape and greatly minimises the risk of clot formation. Having easy, unhindered access to the restroom may be critical for many in terms of the in-flight experience, hence why reserving those usually unpopular aisle seats may be a good idea. Assisted transfer services are available at many airports, and booking this service early is essential. The senior traveller should not be hesitant about asking for help or making their requirements known to airlines in advance. Wheelchairs and mobility carts should be freely available everywhere and are vital to those of compromised mobility to ensure the smooth passage from check-in to the dreaded security, the transfer through which can be more logistically challenging than relocating an aircraft carrier.

General advice to all travellers includes the usual maxim: halve the luggage and double the money. Airlines are becoming stricter in relation to checked-in and carry-on allowances and will start charging for emotional baggage too if given half a chance. Despite some of the aggravations associated with travel for older people, the sheer joy of participating in the technological marvel that is air travel as well as the connections that it affords means that it is vital to keep seniors on the move, as well as everyone else. Accommodating the needs of older people is firmly the responsibility of those who have inherited and profited from the legacy of Orville and Wilbur Wright.

Summer Holidays – The Great Escape

Having done the Houdini and escaped unscathed from the clutches of the life-sapping work environment, retirement, for some, can be like firing a starting gun on a permanent holiday that does not need to be fitted around the demands of work. With no punitive pile of paperwork to return to and with no imminent flight home, the more ambitious vacationer may decide to do something more adventurous than a standard fortnight in Malaga; why not go island hopping in Greece or volunteering in India for a few months? Where is it written that the gap year is the sole preserve of youthful, non-seasoned voyagers? We should live as we would wish to travel: sailing in our boat, with and not against the current of life's opportunities, with no return ticket and with enough bravery to jettison the paddle of caution. The craft that remains in the harbour of life is safe but it is certainly not what boats or their crews were designed for! Surely the greatest mistake any novice retiree can make is to question why holidays are now necessary given the fact that one is no longer so firmly strapped into the strait-jacket of daily work. For many, the biggest retirement goal *is* travelling, surpassing DIY, gardening, and the less riveting hobbies of knitting and crocheting. As the summer beckons and the craving to join the hordes with boarding cards accelerates, what tips, strategies and inspirational ideas do we need to maximise the joy of getting away from it all?

Treasuring the leisure that older people can enjoy in vacationing means first appreciating the lack of constraints that in the past curbed any enthusiasm for spontaneous travel. No longer are older people confined to the peak travel periods of July and August when prices, crowds and temperatures soar. The best time to travel for many is most definitely outside peak season, when your dream trip has the potential to keep giving all year round. The happy coincidence is that you will have to give considerably less to get a great holiday, aided by the fact that one can be flexible on travel dates and can then pick up considerable discounts. If winter is a season that is dreaded because of cold, darkness, dampness and general gloom, what better way to neutralise its negative effects than by following those migrating birds south once in a while? A strategically booked week or two in a sunnier climate in the winter can, for many, stave off the winter blues.

Wherever it is that we call home, it is true to say that if we travel far or near, the world can exhibit overwhelming beauty and diversity as we encounter inspirational, extraordinary and magical experiences. Travel is one of the truly great gifts of modern life, and today's inhabitants of planet earth are the first generation to be able to visit every corner of the world – most destinations being just mere hours away. Being able to travel is not just about strength of sinew, however; it is also about the cash stash, and older retirees may have lump sums specifically earmarked for the personal indulgence of being on the move. The potential impact on our energy levels and enthusiasm for life, never mind our personal happiness in knowing that we have such infinite possibility, is obvious. It could be said that travel for older people is particularly apt, but 'APT' is also a key travel acronym that stands for what should happen before boarding the plane, train or automobile: namely Anticipation, Preparation and the act of Travel itself.

It is said that half the joy of a holiday comes from the process of imaginative speculation about the trip. In an era of instant gratification, enjoyment only truly comes from suffering the pains and pleasures of anticipation and deferral. However we may try to control or prepare for a longed-for trip or how many guide books we read in advance, the joy of travel means invariably that our predictions may only be partially accurate.

An element of preparation for successful travel is undoubtedly important as one gets older, whilst again maintaining a balance to avoid a potentially paralysing sense of too much caution. Technological gadgets that threaten to make travels easier if not totally re-chargeable include a mobile phone, a battery charger and digital camera while two-way walkie-talkies can also prove invaluable if lost in an exotic bazaar or bus station. A digital camera or camera phone can also be used to share photos of your home and family with new acquaintances as well as capturing and reliving the memorable sights and experiences of your trip. A notebook and pen may seem superfluous in a digital era but can be helpful for writing down names and addresses of new-found friends as well as writing a memoir or journal of thoughts, observations and inspirations of the moment during your travels.

It has been said that travel is the only true way to slow down the passage of time as our senses become alive to new experiences and the temporal acceleration that accompanies the more mundane aspects of life is suspended. In the ordinary treadmill of life, successive birthdays come around remarkably quickly, yet twelve months of travel can supply a lifetime of adventure and seems an inordinately long period of time compared to the standard two-week fare. Whatever the motive for travel, the older person ideally wants to come back refreshed, happy, wiser and healthier – all good reasons to escape to a dream destination with our imaginations leading the way!

September

Back to Life's School

September and autumn is first and foremost a season of harvest and abundance when things fatten up and come to fruition. This is not just a reassuring and charitable reframe on an ever-expanding waist-line; the seasonal turning is rich in symbolism for older people as the year enters the youth of its old age, albeit with a jewel-toned golden majesty, and the green of nature turns bronze. Although September may signal the end of summer and a return to the scholastic grindstone for younger people, for others, poignant memories of this transition to autumn are dominated also by schoolyards, but schoolyards of yesteryear. Older people may no longer graze their knees against cage-like desks or be forced to recite endless verses or receive bouquets of newly sharpened pencils, but autumn can subconsciously remind us of a new journey, when many activities restart after the summer break and new challenges present themselves. We have time to reflect on all that we have learned as a result of our life experience and how we learned so much, including those formative, significant years spent in our alma mater. Research conducted in 2015 at University College London has shown that adults aged 35 and above disproportionately recalled experiences in their lives between the ages of 10 and 30 than from any other time, hence why it can be refreshing to stretch those memory muscles and recall those years when so much of our personality was moulded.

Any implication of decline as summer ebbs away must be tempered by the realisation that September is for many people a 'mini' new year, with many activities in society being quietly anchored to the academic homecoming. With the approach of our autumn years and the imminence of winter around the next seasonal corner, it is truly wondrous within the twilight of autumn to be presented with a fresh start. One of the great strategies in later life is to recognise and embrace these fresh beginnings rather than bemoaning that which withers away.

Autumn is a season for the senses – a time of spectacular colours and tastes as nature's bounty is harvested. Although we may sense a drop in the temperature and the leaves falling reminds us that the natural world is edging towards dormancy, autumn remains a season without the pests of spring and summer. We no longer have to contend with the flies, mosquitoes, weeds and psychological baggage of our earlier years, which can all be gracefully left behind as we mature with the seasons. It is poignant to savour the waning days of light and warmth as the long days of summer take a final bow. It is akin to savouring the last drops of a fine wine or slowly lingering over the last bites of a sumptuous meal that we don't want to end. While Autumn arrives on summer's heels, it is not without a warm glow of its own as it urges us to harvest the abundance and sweetness of life. Occasionally we can pause in the putting away of the croquet sets when the harvest weather provides an unexpected bounty in the form of an Indian summer. Autumn, like other seasons if we liken life to the divisions of the year, also allows for planting, growth and flowering; is not just a transitory stage before the aches and pains of winter.

The relief of many older people is palpable when the services they rely on, such as day centres and active retirement groups, resume after the summer break. Autumn can afford the opportunity to enrol in adult education classes, be they baby-boomer boogie lessons, courses in pumpkin carving or photography. Friendships may be quite randomly forged during September, as in our youth, depending on whose desk or table you shared. Although some may sense a mortality gradually unfurling beneath them, others can see the opportunity to acquire new skills, recasting a more vibrant image of themselves whilst expanding their personal and social horizons.

A deeper understanding of the meaning of life can also become apparent as we enter the autumnal years. The challenge is to discover and experience a quieter phase of existence, to grow beyond an outward focus and develop a deeper, quieter consciousness, allowing new voices and wisdom to help us appreciate both the subtle and the sublime. This inward orientation is not a narcissistic self-preoccupation but a challenging voyage of self-renewal. It can allow us stand more comfortably on the edge of the unknown, to be less dogmatic, and more observant, appreciative and creative than we may have ever thought possible. The artist, writer and poet may emerge in us, finding new voices and giving expressions to a bountiful harvest as we bask in the contented glow of autumn. The things we have laboured over so intensely in the earlier phases of life begin to pay dividends for us and those around us. We may have reared children to adulthood, acquired and developed new friendships, displayed time-acquired wisdom and a deep knowledge of our chosen professions. These harvest gifts grow, sometimes unnoticed, over a lifetime, but we must continue to appreciate and savour this sweet elixir by applying generous amounts of wisdom, love and gratitude. Within our community, older people can be truly authentic ambassadors for the autumn years, not content to shelter under the mature canopy but striving to build an even greater and richer harvest.

A Season of Gratitude

September is the time to notice that our cup of life's elixir may not only be half full but permanently teeming to the brim if we allow our inner gaze to actually notice the glass in the first place, as well as perceiving the richness of its contents. September gives us the chance to ditch the diatribe of disapproval about modern living and to reap life's many rewards rather than grumbling about the aches, pains and enforced change of later years. It can be all too easy to ooze pessimism and ruminate on the rheumatoid and other ailments once a certain age is reached. The immortal words 'It wasn't like that in my day' may seem like a mantra for those belonging to a rose-tinted mindset. We should also recall the many generations before ours who have been where we are today without any of the conveniences we enjoy – most of us no longer have to grow our food, carry water every day or travel miles on foot just to carry a message or share the latest gossip with a friend. The conveniences and technologies of today have given us much more time to spend on the activities we enjoy, whether this is kicking piles of autumn leaves along forested paths or following the breath trails from our grandchildren as they kick footballs along soon-to-be-frosted pitches. For this, we can choose to be supremely grateful.

Gratitude can be thought of as an appreciation of life's good things as well as the recognition of the struggles of living. Boosting the mood-batteries has never been more challenging in modern society where expectations are high and entitlements are vigorously sought. The cognitive skill-set of gratitude calls for an awareness of the privileges and pleasures of living as well as the mindful acceptance of the challenges inherent in our daily existence. As mindsets go, a statement that life is fundamentally worthwhile regardless of circumstances is highly adaptive and can help us avoid excessive depression. Let's face it – you can't be grateful and miserable simultaneously, so a demeanour of gratitude can really improve our quality of life. If we allow a natural instinct of gratitude to be inhibited or devalued and instead aim for ever-greater material gratification, we run the risk of perpetual resentment, disappointment and worry. Oprah Winfrey knew the limitations and benefits of material possessions when she reflected 'Though I am grateful for the blessings of wealth, it hasn't changed who I am. My feet are still firmly on the ground. I'm just wearing better shoes'.

Whenever something happens that seems to initially represent a setback, it may turn out later to be a seminal moment that actually set us up for greater development, learning and self-awareness. Rather than mindlessly chasing the proverbial thirty pieces of silver, all we have to do is see the silver linings amidst the dark clouds that float into our horizons from time to time. Gratitude should not only come to the surface during times of joy but also at times of very human struggle, when courage and resilience facilitate victories that are hard-earned but savoured. A mindset of gratitude also helps us build emotional reserves. Even if we can't be grateful for what we have received, we can and should be thankful for what we have escaped. For the independent-minded older person who preciously guards their self-image, a fixed mental attitude of gratitude is no threat to self-assuredness as gratitude has nothing to do with needing charity from others or having a lack of assertiveness or ambition. The spiritual act of finding and expressing gratitude, of praising the bridge that carries us over, is in fact empowering. It allows us to paint any adversity into a finer landscape whilst wisely taking nothing for granted.

The French philosopher Jacques Maritain in *Reflections on America* (1958) cited the need to not only feel gratitude but also to express it, stating that 'Gratitude is the most exquisite form of courtesy ... but feeling it and not expressing it is like wrapping a present and not giving it.' Silent gratitude is of little use to anyone but openly expressed appreciation helps the donor and recipient feel more positive, relish the good experiences, preserve old friendships and procure new ones. If we also record a daily journal of events, we can become more mindful of the present and also aware of what our possible future self would look like. A gratitude diary, diligently compiled, can make the art of expressing gratitude a more natural response in many situations, even in difficult circumstances such as loss and bereavement. Being grateful for the gift of a life or time spent with a loved one can help to melt away the most acute grief.

Are older people better placed to express their appreciation than the younger generation in the face of unexpected kindness or the benevolence of life? Cynics may claim that the young acknowledge instances of kindness in anticipation of repeated favours while only the old and wise grow through their expressed gratitude, seeing the need to not only return kindness to immediate benefactors but also to leave a wider legacy. Gratitude powerfully begets more gratitude, thus expanding our powers of observation, happiness and appreciation. The exhortation of G.K. Chesterton when asked to join in a grace before meals was to include grace before the concert, opera, pantomime, walking, playing, before a book is opened and before a paintbrush is used. Gratitude is, claimed Cicero, the parent of all other virtues.

Thirty Days Has September – Cool Ways to Remember

When we forget the odd name or two or venture upstairs only to fail to recall the purpose of our ascent as soon as we put our foot on the last stair, we may begin to worry that something is wrong with our memory, especially if these incidents happen often. We are surrounded by technology that has revolutionised the way we keep track of many of life's details, trivial or otherwise. Appliances turn themselves on and off (unlike humans, who may desire but can never quite obtain an on-button equivalent); phones (which are a lot smarter than their owners), laptops and tablets remind us of appointments and phone numbers; while Google and other search engines allows us to search for all the information in the world. Still we grow frustrated and anxious when words fail to arrive on the tips of our tongues, when we misplace items, when we forget to write those important cheques on grandchildren's birthdays or when we fail to retrieve appointments and directions. Cruelly, all this may occur for many who otherwise feel quite cerebrally accomplished, with plenty of accumulated wisdom and knowledge of the world. Sadly, it seems to be the case that just as one's head is beginning to be put together correctly, the memory and the body begin to fall apart. Although the word 'amnesia' sounds faintly reassuring, like a cross between milk of magnesia and ambrosia, it can imply a progressive descent into a serious illness. Is there another interpretation of these so-called 'senior moments', and can older people do anything to defy the decline in the fluid mechanics of the brain?

Anyone paying a nostalgic nod to their inner teenager will recall nail-biting times when they stayed up until the early hours cramming their heads with facts and equations, never to be encountered in the real world but required to be accurately regurgitated onto paper in order to ascend the academic greasy pole. Many will also recall waking the next morning to discover that same recall then deserting them in the eerie silence of a draughty exam hall, when their entire brain seems empty of all useful information. Such agony illustrates that clueless moments, however charming, are not the sole preserve of older members of society; temporary lapses of memory afflict us all, particularly when we are stressed or anxious. Many, if not most, of the common cognitive errors occurring in later life have nothing to do with their most catastrophic interpretation, namely dementia or Alzheimer's disease. While we do admittedly tend to lose out on the neuronal or brain cell-count over time, neuroscientists now believe that the decline in the numbers of nerve cells is less than previously thought, and networks of nerve cells compensate by communicating more readily with each other to eventually accomplish the same task. For example, when we were young we could push a car with one hand; as we age we may need two hands to push the car as our physical strength is reduced: the same result is achieved, albeit with less speed, but perhaps with more precision and accuracy. The removal of surplus brain cells can, moreover, bring some benefits, similar to clearing the garage of old paint pots. The space you have left to work in is a lot less cluttered, leaving your remaining intellectual tools easier to spot and use more creatively. It is now also believed that certain key brain regions governing judgement, insight and reflective ability continue to expand well into middle age. Little wonder that older people who remain mentally active can consistently outperform younger competitors – and not just in competitions to recall old Van Morrison lyrics or in singing all the words of Leonard Cohen ballads! It has long been observed in the Open University that the best results are consistently achieved by those in the 60 to 65 age group. We also know that older people are more reliable on tasks of prospective memory than their younger (hungover) counterparts, and if asked to undertake a future task at a set time, they will do so with greater fidelity. Would-be extended holiday-makers beware, therefore, if you are relying on younger offspring to water houseplants, feed the cat or clean the fish tank.

It is indeed reassuring to note that there are many tips, tricks and techniques to train our memory as we drag information from the back of our minds to the tips of our tongues. One can use a wide range of memory devices or mnemonics – some are mental short cuts, others are catchy rhymes and silly jokes, but all can succeed in sending quick reminders to the brain. Other techniques include writing information down, creating a catchword or phrase for that especially memorable quote or witty retort that usually only comes to us on the bus on the way home. Altering something strategically in the environment to trigger a reminder can be useful and reviewing details in advance can keep those appointments handy, thus helping to outsmart even the densest fog of amnesia. It has been said many times that the best way to deal with mild memory loss is the use of memory aids and strategies, as described above, coupled with a good sense of humour. In a competitive world that seems to place cognitive function and intellectual ability higher on the social desirability scale than the absence of cellulite or wrinkles, a decline in memory can be a cause of considerable alarm, conjuring up images of nursing homes and adult-sized diapers. This in turn can lead to understandably intense dissatisfaction, which prompts many to wish that they could go back to their youth. Only the erudite elderly who are brimming with senior sagacity will know the best intellectual deterrent to this wish that is also a highly challenging memory exercise largely confined to but equally repugnant to the young: algebra.

September Surprise – A Love Harvest

In Ireland's County Clare, September is marked by the start of one of Europe's largest matchmaking festivals, when the town of Lisdoonvarna woos up to 60,000 visitors from home and abroad for its month-long festival of romance. The population of this spa town for the rest of the year comes in at approximately 800 residents who have played host to romantic hopefuls, bachelor farmers and accompanying revellers for the last 150 years. The arrival of high-velocity speed dating and other online temptations of the interpersonal kind hasn't quelled the need for the services of the matchmaker, with age being no barrier to participation in the rituals of passion and conviviality. Rumour has it that the older rather than the younger participants are the first to dance and the last to leave the sessions with their heady mix of music, drink and general merriment. In a society that is slow to acknowledge that older people need or can obtain a soulmate or love interest, it is truly refreshing to see older people who are willing to push out the boundaries of love.

One of the many misconceptions and myths surrounding later life is the view that old age is loveless and lonely and that withdrawing from all things romantic is a social necessity. There is a common perception that, while the older generation do dignity and reserve, intimacy and displays of affection are only for young adults; thus, discussion of the need for, and overt expression of, romantic love in older people has acquired the status of a taboo topic. This prejudice may unfortunately feed into a general belief that many of life's doors (particularly the bedroom's) close as we grow older, as can many other opportunities. In a society that has become desensitised to many forms of sexual imagery and champions equality of opportunity for homosexual persons in relation to access to marriage and civil partnership, it is somewhat ironic that sexual expression in older people is seen as disgusting, comical or both. Surely only the most narrow-minded of us, however, would expect all who are neither young nor physically attractive to be eternally asexual. The pharmaceutical industry has deliberately fired a love arrow in the direction of older people and perhaps unwittingly helped to slay the prejudice against older eroticism by marketing products such as Viagra to the general public. It is not only the profits of corporations such as Pfizer that have soared as a result, but also undoubtedly the libidinous aspirations of many an older lover.

Whereas the young equate and indeed confuse love with sexual activity, it is only the more mature who realise that sex is not an essential exertion in enduring romantic relationships, the essence of which is surely the emotional attachment. While older love is entitled to and claims its share of sparks and fireworks, when the pyrotechnics are finished the calmer waters of mature love help the flow of a more caring and reciprocal connection. Romance in our younger and middle years may be hindered by the anxieties of managing fertility, the hustle and bustle of daily life and the interruption of curious children. There is no doubt that some physical activities do find limitations in old age, but that emotional need for a special affinity with a soulmate or life partner remains. A love life is perfectly capable of rejuvenation in later years and can flourish without the limiting factors of time-juggling between children and careers. In the most unlikely setting of nursing and residential homes, even when management looks upon intimacy between seniors as a problem, friendship and love can blossom in surroundings where unlimited conversation and emotional sharing occurs. The more imaginative of us could possibly compare a good nursing home to an extended summer camp where crushes, infatuations and sleep-away romances abound. Even when things get serious, it's not always about an emphasis on emotion over libido. An accumulated mileage on the clock of life will also imply a certain inner confidence and ability to be comfortable with yourself, which means you know what you want sexually and are unafraid to ask for it. Letting go of the vanity and multi-layered inhibitions of youth is surely one of the most refreshing aspects of growing old. This hopefully allows us to reach a state of peace with our less-than-perfect bodies. The ability to love truly has no age limit, regardless of whether the object of our affections is someone new or a cherished and committed life partner.

As always, as the latter years of life approach and the cooler breeze of mortality is felt, the issue of a love legacy looms larger. How can we pass on the lessons in love we have learned on life's journey? Do we have insights to share in a diary or journal to pass on to the next generation as a treasure trove of insight about the nature of love, marriage and enduring friendship? Special memories of a spouse, partner, children, family and friends are both equally precious and fleeting but require expression and faithful recording to convey our unique take on life and love. The call of September and the matchmaking season should thus lead us to recapture the sense of romance within ourselves by caring, sharing, observing and conversing. An inspiring role model in affairs of the heart is surely the great American artist Georgia O'Keeffe, who, at 84, hooked up with a 27-year-old potter and, ignoring her notoriety, travelled the world while remaining invigorated in life and art by her young flame. This was only extinguished when Georgia left this world and her young lover at the age of 98.

OCTOBER

International Day for Older Persons

During a United Nations assembly in 1990, the UN officially declared 1 October as the International Day for Older Persons in recognition of the contributions older people have made and to highlight and examine the issues affecting their lives. For participants in the workplace, this day is sadly not a public holiday but is instead an important global observance. The 1 October is first and foremost about giving seniors a collective pat on the back for their efforts and the value brought to society. As a result of this, people are standing up against ageism and intergenerational resentment. This defuses the ticking bomb of prejudicial, negative attitudes toward the older members of society. The question remains, however, if an appreciation day is the best way to counter pubescent prejudice from a cohort that has a passion for regarding their elders as senile. Should older people stand their ground in society as mainstream citizens rather than enduring its patronising praise and platitudes?

It has been said that a true test of society is how it treats those in the dawn of life (children), the twilight of life (older people) and those who live in the shadows of life (such as the sick, needy or those with a disability). The International Day for Older Persons, if it does nothing else for the collective morale of a generation, would do well to challenge, identify and question ageist attitudes and to understand the impact these attitudes have on people themselves. We now know that the virus of ageism infects most people in most countries around the world. We have also come to realise that when older adults internalize the negative stereotypes, from the corrosive humour of 'geezer' jokes to the assumption that inadequacy and bodily failures are inevitable as we cross ageing milestones, it can affect their own healthy functioning. More worryingly, stereotypes that underpin ageism contribute to widespread discrimination against older people in the workplace, the medical care system and even within families. Even for those who push the humour boundaries, they are at risk of unwittingly mocking an entire segment of society for the sake of a cheap laugh, which essentially legitimises and normalises ageist discrimination in the process. Erdman Palmore of Duke University conducted a survey on this topic, and 58 percent of respondents reported that they experienced ageism by being at the receiving end of jokes poking fun at the bladder-control problems, forgetfulness and hair loss associated with old age. Humour associated with ageing has remained fair game for years, perhaps due to the universality of ageing, the contradiction of mocking one's future self and the license it gives us to have fun with noxious stereotypes. A code of conduct for the greetings card industry would not go astray here, focusing on promoting celebratory messages for those all-important round-number birthdays, rather than adding another brick to the wall of ageism with all its harmful effects.

Because of the ubiquitous presence of ageism, it remains the most socially normalised of any prejudice, and is not widely disputed, like racism and sexism. It remains an everyday challenge for older people who are overlooked for employment opportunities, restricted from social services, stereotyped in the media and marginalised from many areas of society. Tragically, but in many ways predictably, older people absorb these negative attitudes and respond by reducing their expectations of themselves and settling for less from life. More worryingly, these negative attitudes are directly linked with premature mortality. In Becca Levy's 2002 study, the Yale psychologist found that those who had negative self-perceptions of ageing lived 7.5 years less than those who had positive self-perceptions of ageing. It is as if older people are blind to their own achievements and how they can contribute to society through voluntary work, the transmission of experience through formal and informal mentoring, helping their own families with caring responsibilities and even participating in the labour market.

The thorny issue of intergenerational relations and age discrimination, which can make seniors useful scapegoats for collective social problems, is another potentially sinister by-product of ageism. There is an age-old accusation, perhaps fostered to an extent by economists, that older people are sucking the young dry and draining the resources away from education, failing to sacrifice their jobs and assets in order to allow younger hopefuls have their turn. The reality 'on the ground' in relation to contact between generations and mutual expectations of each other is an overriding sense of interconnectedness and mutual dependency, despite the lack of respect and accommodation for the participation of older people in society. There is a need for a fostering of common ground between young and old to address this deficit in positive perceptions of ageing. Otherwise older people face exclusion, often on the grounds of being if not unproductive then distinctly unattractive as they 'make the place ugly' with wrinkles and blemishes of age. We need solidarity and respect between generations with the promotion of optimal role models for each age cohort if generations are to understand and learn from each other. It should behove the young to listen to the old, not because they are always right but because they have much more experience of being wrong. The reality is that a little grey hair is a small price to pay for all that accumulated wisdom.

The challenge of the intergenerational relationship must be to awaken the passion and creativity of youth, and combine it with the wisdom, experience and insight of older people in the quest to improve the world. It is true that when youth takes the initiative, they will lead their elders in new directions and ask questions that dare not be asked.

Above all, a day honouring older people is not only in the form of privileges such as extra chores being done or treats delivered. The day is also about realising a fundamental respect for people who for many years have left aside what they inherited and are reaping rewards from what they have earned.

World Mental Health Day

World Mental Health Day, which falls on the 10 of October every year, raises awareness about and acknowledges our most precious entity: an individual's mental well-being. Society's negative stereotyping of older people often implies that older people are especially vulnerable to attrition in this area, be it from the ravages of dementia or the apparent melancholy associated with old age. The fight to challenge these stereotypes certainly wasn't helped by the utterances of psychological gurus like Sigmund Freud, who stated that 'Near or above the age of fifty the elasticity of the mental processes as a rule is lacking [....] old people are no longer educable.' Although Freud later retracted this statement (presumably to justify charging the older attendees of his lectures who were eager to learn and were coincidentally richer than your average impoverished student), it was a cruel blow nonetheless to the collective morale of older people. Old age thereby remained a relatively unexplored territory for the psychoanalytic disciples of Freud, who may have been deterred from studying the evolution of later life by his ageist attitude and instead devoted their energies to more youthful conundrums and concerns such as the science behind potty training and tantrum-throwing.

While Freud may have smeared an entire generation and expressed prejudice against his future self, other psychologists such as Eric Erikson speculated that human maturation extended well into later life (as mothers knew all along, especially where their ostensibly grown-up but still umbilically attached sons were concerned) and so, one could mention words like growth and old age in the same sentence without appearing in need of long-term psychiatric incarceration. Old age is not just about decay and decline, nor is it inevitable that one's mental health fractures and fragments as we become older. In contrast to the body, which stops growing in early adulthood, research from the Oregon University's Brain Institute suggests that the brain continues to grow and expand well into middle age. The external features of the skull such as those delinquent eyelids, uneven ear lobes, yellow teeth and a hairline in full surrender threaten to reveal the extent of chronological assault on the external body more than on the brain and the mind.

It is also worth noting that not every mental faculty declines with age; some intellectual attributes such as wisdom and one's vocabulary actually improve. In my clinical experience some mental illnesses such as anxiety disorders either rarely present themselves or actually get better as we age, as is the case with lifelong schizophrenia. Emotional baggage that played havoc with our earlier years can get unpacked and stored away for good, thus less likely to sabotage our successes, triumphs and ambitions. That unreasonable inner critic that judged us more harshly than any fossilised member of the judiciary can finally be silenced for good.

Nor is old age synonymous with major depression or getting lost in a vale of tears, even if the mist from an occasional cataract threatens to obscure one's ocular and psychological vision. While youngsters may need to 'throw a sickie' or take 'a mental health day' to evaluate why they are still working and cracking under everyday stress, most older people face the challenges of life with equanimity, good humour, fortitude and courage. Being buffeted by bereavement, sickness and other losses, many veterans of life take pride in their eventual ability to manage life-transitions and unexpected stresses with resilience, resourcefulness and hardiness. Physical limitations may at times threaten to take over one's mind but never one's funny bone; humour and zest allows adaptation to many frailties, however unwelcome they may seem initially. Even if our physical stamina wanes or our free movement is inhibited by pain, it is a myth to imply that our vitality progressively leeches away with every passing year. The reality is that we never lose our former selves as we age. In relation to our mental attributes and resources, our personal biography and rich life experiences continue to be added to with every passing year. The perspective of age also can bestow an emotional freedom as the inessentials of life get sloughed off. With increased age comes psychological maturity; we know what we want out of life and we become more comfortable in our skin, even if it is lined with more laughter than worry lines.

While the majority of older people continue to rate their quality of life as good until their mid-eighties, if an illness such as major depression does arise for the first time in later life, the condition (along with many other mental illnesses) responds just as well to treatment as it does in younger adults. Young and old alike will agree that antidepressants work best if taken when the water is lapping near one's hammock on a Caribbean beach. Being a pessimist by nature isn't a prerequisite to developing clinical depression either; many a depressed optimist has temporarily succumbed to the melancholy bug only to bounce back, once immunity from stress and a laid-back attitude to life has been restored. The good news for those who jealously safeguard their mental health as we age is that later life is not just about the mind forgetting and the mirror reminding: the more recent generations of older people are more proactively in charge of their own mental health and well-being than ever before.

Oktoberfest – Keep Calm and Prost On

Oktoberfest is a magical time for those who are besotted with beer and sausage meat. This German import that has arrived in our towns and cities has become part of a larger fiesta of celebrations during the latter part of October that culminates in Halloween. Apart from the appearance of more beer in more places and the arrival of crisp autumn weather, does a festival in October generate any interest for an older generation who have come to realise the limitations of overindulgence and indeed the dangers of trying the fifty shades of drunk? The statistics behind the Bavarian festival, established in 1810, are indeed staggering, almost certainly along with the participants themselves, due in no small measure to the approximately 7.7 million litres of beer that are consumed annually in Munich during Oktoberfest. It seems the Bavarians took the expressed sentiments of the great American patriot Benjamin Franklin to their hearts and livers when he reputedly said that 'Beer is proof that God loves us and wants us to be happy'. A sixteen-day folk festival to celebrate the drawing in of grain might, at first glance, seem to sedately avoid the concentrated and frenetic over-indulgence of a rock concert or other juvenile festival. However, the tumultuous party atmosphere of Oktoberfest has led to, among other restrictions placed some years ago, an official curbing of the afternoon music to 85 decibels, specifically to preserve the beer-tent atmosphere for older folks and their families. If older people are officially on the guestlist, what rules of engagement are necessary for the preservation of all-round dignity in the midst of alcoholic substances that have been helping people lower their standards since time immemorial?

It is generally recognised that wine improves with age, but is the converse true? You could be forgiven for thinking yes, given the availability and number of wine appreciation courses available as standard classroom fare, often being promoted as an integral part of the adult learning and education courses directed at retirees. Wine appreciation

Declan Lyons

is reputedly 'a vast and ever-changing world that offers the devotee almost unlimited scope for exploration, contemplation and social contact' according to Ted Heybridge, author of *The Joy of Retirement: For Those Who Live Life to the Full*, who is a great advocate of wine discovery programmes. Alcohol is frequently described in glowing terms such as 'a well-earned pint' or 'a cool glass of wine while relaxing with family and friends'. When you have all the time in the world on your hands, why not repeatedly fill it (and your glass) to the brim with the magical social elixir? Alcohol allegedly has the ability to render the imbiber virtually omnipotent with its propensity to make you see double and feel single. Sadly, other potencies and virtues can wane in direct parallel with the quantity imbibed, irrespective of one's age. Nonetheless, 'the clamour for a beaker of wine to wet one's mind and say something clever' according to Aristophanes, the comic playwright, is as strong as ever. There are even some older people who claim that a beer-run fulfils their weekly exercise requirements, although we all know that the only muscles likely to be exercised in the process of drinking are those attached to the elbow joint.

Whether we retain the same drinking habits from our youth or not, there is no doubt that our bodies change; our corporeal tolerance for alcohol and our ability to metabolise it plunges, and for many, over-indulgence and it's after-effects are less cool as we grow older. Harmful drinking in seniors can be associated with greater safety concerns such as falls, accidents, episodes of confusion, chest infections and heart failure that may result in a need for acute medical care and hospitalisation. There is an old saying among clinicians in the field that alcohol can harm every organ system in the body, from the top of the head to the tips of one's toes. Public awareness of liver cirrhosis may be high, and whilst people acknowledge that heavy drinking may expel a few functional brain cells from active service here and there, few are aware that alcohol may be a contributor to memory and cognitive decline as a prelude to dementia. The harmful use of alcohol is also strongly associated with depression and anxiety, and the connections between alcohol addiction and major depression are well known. If depression is an unwelcome squatter in one's abode, alcohol can be seen as its unbidden roommate. Loneliness, isolation, personal bereavement, sudden redundancy or retirement can all feel like good reasons for reaching for the bottle. Oftentimes, families, friends and even health-care workers overlook concerns about drinking in older people, seeing it as an understandable reaction to the vicissitudes of life. Amongst the young, alcohol abuse is a visible social disorder whereas drinking when one is older generally occurs at home, below the radar of public concern.

When should an older person become concerned about their drinking? Enthusiasm to procure it may be a warning sign and returning from a continental holiday with one's car boot rattling with the sounds of nice bottles of Merlot can make the hopefully sober driver a target for the health police, if not the breathalyzer. The recommended amount of alcohol units are a definite clue, and the more one deviates from recommended weekly limits, the more likely you are to attract the label of a harmful drinker. The sad reality for some is that older people should probably consume a lot less than the recommended maximum of 14 units of alcohol a week for healthy adult women and 21 units for men. Some experts advise that 7 units per week should be the maximum consumption, bearing in mind that a glass of cranberry juice is likely to contain far more antioxidants than the equivalent volume of wine. For those who find that alcohol is becoming increasingly indispensable or who refuse to attend their grandchildren's school fundraiser unless they sell liquor, abstinence or controlled social drinking may be the only answer. Picking up a hobby or interest can help fill the void, but we mustn't be put off by those who claim that the worst part of quitting drinking is the lack of excuses you now have for your behaviour. So, this Oktoberfest, moderation is the maxim – the alternative may be turning off the lights and taking the battery out of the doorbell until October is over. Before we miss the party, we need to remember that sobriety can be taken in moderation too.

Halloween – A Time of Tricks and Treats

Straddling the line between autumn and winter; between the harvest bounty and the bleak emptiness of the dark season; and even between life and death itself, Halloween has it all, being a time of both celebration and superstition. Halloween is an annual occasion still observed on the 31 October, which is the eve of the Western Christian feast of All Hallows Day, which marks the start of the period of remembrance of the dead. Halloween as a festival, however, has origins from earlier pagan times with the Celtic feast of Samhain, when the ghosts of the dead were supposed to mingle with the living on the eve of winter. The tradition of Halloween is very much alive today, albeit with heavy commercial trappings. It is the second largest commercial holiday in the United States with an estimated annual spend of six billion dollars. What has Halloween got to offer the older generation who are continually expected to hand out candies and other emblematic treats to their ostensibly adult kids? Is there a time when one is simply too old to trick or treat, or is there an opportunity to magnify the mystique of old age by harnessing the supernatural and the occult?

On the surface, Halloween has a capacity to send a shiver down the collective older spine with its noisy fireworks, ghoulish disguises and menacing costumes converting even the most innocent child into a truly morbid minor. Added to this eerie spectacle is canine apoplexy and other forms of terror that many pets endure as they are traumatised by the noise of low-level explosive pyrotechnics. Seniors could be forgiven for sealing up mailboxes, bunkering down and prematurely hibernating during this freakish festival. It may seem at times as if all hell is about to break loose when the veil between the spiritual and the real world thins and monsters, goblins and ghouls parade down familiar streets they once thought predictable and safe. Some older people may also feel a distinct social pressure to uphold the supposed gentle image of the older generation by not slamming doors or failing to respond in the face of a constant stream of children eliciting endless treats, even when the treats are long gone. Faced with a stalled sweet line, the youth of today are unlikely to be satiated by apples and nuts, and doling out hard cash may be the only way to nip guilt pangs in the bud and avoid seeing juvenile disappointment spread amongst those fresh countenances. Dipping into one's cash stash may additionally be the only way to avoid the social stigma of being labelled as the neighbourhood miser. Halloween can thus be said to come with multiple health, well-being, financial and sanity warnings.

On the other hand, we also need to remind ourselves that the kids are only in costume and one's own inner demons are likely to pose a greater threat than any Halloween freak show. Older people need to confront and deliberate upon a fundamental choice that has to be made: to have the stereotype of fear and vulnerability reinforced, however unintentionally, or to shed the cloak of trepidation, join the party and engage with the fun of Halloween. Halloween allows people of all ages to express a little of their outrageous side and be less inhibited – it can be great fun dressing up as the hero or villain of one's choice. Such self-expression in a communal event can be a vital outlet for those with pathological shyness or social phobia. Physical health, if not perhaps one's heartrate, stands to benefit during Halloween as a result of all that pumpkin ingestion (those edible orange monsters are reputedly high in fibre, potassium and even the eyesight-boosting beta-carotene). There is also exercise to be had in escorting hordes of little ones between your neighbour's houses, not to mention the other fringe benefit: a rare and legitimate excuse to drop in unannounced on your neighbours – the days of stepping through a permanently open and inviting front door to borrow the proverbial cup of sugar are sadly part of community folklore.

Sharing tradition between generations and firing up imaginations with stories of ghosts and ghouls is at the essence of communication between grandchildren and grandparents. What better way for children to learn how to manage and even have fun through fear, than from older and wiser folk who have no vested interest in pretending to be absolutely fearless in every situation? Older people are living repositories of oral story-telling, tradition and wisdom and deserve the exalted status this confers. The young also need to be continually reminded that not all information about human history and endeavour can be collated upon a spreadsheet or digitally regurgitated through a Google search. An affliction of modern living must be the difficulty experienced while sifting through tons of information in the search for that which represents fundamental truth, yet that which is to be found in the hearts and memories of older people connects us with the past in a more authentic way.

Whether we view Halloween as a mere excuse for a party, a boost to the local economy, an ancient Celtic festival, or a complete nuisance to be avoided at all costs, the festival has managed to survive and grow as a secular event with deep spiritual roots whilst transcending religious and ethnic divides – above all, it is a shared celebration between young and old.

NOVEMBER

Cultivate Spirit

November's chills remind us of the whirlwind of winter activities to come and the need to prepare for Christmas as the frost, end-of-season gatherings and cosy indoor spaces beckon. As the autumn decays and the festivities of Halloween fizzle out like a dampened firework, older people may ruefully reflect on yet another year that is slipping by. They can also become aware of a less frenetic perpetual order and ancient mythology where time loses all meaning and the past, present and future merges into one. The ancient Celtic feast of Samhain, which falls on 1 November, marked the division of the year between the lighter half of the year (summer) and the darker half of the year (winter). During Samhain, the ancient Celts believed that the division between this world and the other was at its thinnest, which allowed spirits to pass through.

This festival is not about celebrating thinness in general, however, or about lighting bonfires for other vanities such as meticulously crafted or stretch-mark-free bodies. It is about inviting ancestral spirits to permeate that narrow membrane of our existence by warding off more harmful supernatural beings. Christian tradition incorporated the honouring of the dead into the Christian calendar with All Saints Day (All Hallows Day) on 1 November, followed by All Souls Day on 2 November. The perceptible decline in the sun's strength was an acute source of anxiety for early man who lit fires (the sun's earthly counterpart) in an attempt to assist the sun on its journey across the skies and no doubt to hasten its return for the start of the new year. It is interesting to note that pyromania was socially acceptable in other cultures. The Hindu Diwali festival, marking the start of the Hindu New Year, has been celebrated for generations. Diwali, which shares bonfires and more than a flying spark or two in common with Samhain, its Celtic equivalent, is more optimistically known as the Festival of Light. Has

November anything to offer the older generation or is it just about lighting dark spaces and avoiding the cold? Are there inherent benefits in becoming a spiritual major-leaguer at the start of life's winter?

The beginning of winter serves to remind us how far we have come along our journey, whether through this year or during a long life. We may not have succeeded in all our goals or achieved public fame and fortune, but stellar individual achievements such as family and work accomplishments can be consolidated and personal challenges reflected upon. November could be thus themed as a self-appreciation month; it being the second-last month of the year also allows us to pick up the pace in achieving any outstanding goals and increasing our self-knowledge. Cultivating our spirit and developing spiritual awareness becomes increasingly important in later life, despite rampant secularism in the rest of modern society. If spirit is the non-physical part of a person, the seat of emotions and deeper soulful character, the quest for harmony between body and spirit must get easier as the spirit finally catches up with and even eclipses the body that moves a little less frenetically. An invincible sense of spirit can thus enter a human being and dwell there undisturbed in the relative stillness of later life. It could be argued that sickness and ageing represent the body's inability to reach the natural goal of unity with the mind and spirit. While on one hand this may seem a dispiriting failure, on the other it can be a clarion call to do more with our lives before illness reminds us that our time is finite: the one reality we must accept is that, apart from taxation, life has a definite date of expiration. Having duly sucked the morrow from life's bone, it is our spirit that helps us realise that all is not yet lost.

The other meaning of spirit, apart from the favourite splash of highly concentrated liquid we may consume from a shot glass, refers to the repository of life knowledge, tradition and wisdom that helps age-proof the souls of many older people. Since ancient times, people have kept history alive by performing old rituals and traditions, often with the central participation of elders. A call to our ancestors for guidance and inspiration can settle timid hearts and strengthen the resolve of those in the midst of any crisis. For a world captivated by high speed and instant gratification, people's fascination with history, relics and antiques seems strangely disconnected from modernity but it is also essential for connecting with and celebrating our human identity and heritage. Being old is about being authentic, genuinely valuable and beautiful. Although the steps of some seniors may be slow, they need not be without purpose as younger generations still follow and older people still lead, even up to the last lap of life's journey. It is still relevant for older people to ask themselves whether they are leading victoriously or have they surrendered some of their spirit and independence along the way. However we brand or individualise our inner spirit, whether it's a feisty humour, a quiet and gentle dignity or an insatiable curiosity, the legacy of life lessons we leave transmit that essence of our spirit to the next generation.

Remember in November

As the winter season begins, the days draw darker, shorter and colder, much to the discomfort of many an ageing body. The period of winter is a good time for useful, active introspection to remember those who have passed away and how they have contributed to our lives. The venerable tradition of praying for the dead can take many forms including visiting cemeteries and making offerings and prayers as the barriers between humans and their ancestors fade as the dead become more accessible, especially during All Saints Day and All Souls Day. This is far from a morbid exercise, as this respect is based on the premise that we are all the result of a thousand loves. It is also reassuring for those who have waded through life's choppy waters to know that they will be remembered for their noble endeavours despite having journeyed to the next world. November can thus be a month of reflection and celebration, when older people defy the stereotype that they're incapable of remembering anything.

It was Mark Twain who said in 'The War Prayer', published after his death in 1910, that 'Remembrance is a great focus of patriotism, which is about supporting your country all the time and your government when it deserves it.' Veterans' Day in the United States and Remembrance Day in the United Kingdom falls annually on 11 November, which is the anniversary of the signing of the armistice that ended the First World War. Veterans of other conflicts whose sacrifice was the pinnacle of their patriotism are also acknowledged on this day. With the technological advances in warfare, perhaps there should be an additional memorial day to honour all the brave drones lost in combat in more recent times. Most seniors feel passionately about honouring living veterans, whether still on active duty, discharged, retired or in the reserve as people who at one point in their life wrote a blank cheque made payable to their country for an amount up to and including their life. On Remembrance Day, however, it is not just the combatants who are honoured. There also were (and are) those who emerged from the trenches as writers and poets, who started preaching peace and who made this world a kinder place in which to live. For many reasons, therefore, older servicemen and servicewomen may experience a profound morale boost on Remembrance Day as they embody national pride, lay aside old bitterness and display a fraction of the spirit that enabled them to face mortal danger when an imperilled nation required them to do their duty. They may not have had any idea of the value of these formative moments until they became memories, yet the effects of their courage and fortitude reverberates through future generations.

November may also provide a useful and necessary opportunity to intercede on behalf of those faithful departed who have departed earthly life but who, according to some Christian traditions, have not yet reached the joy of heaven and remain immobilised in the waiting room of Purgatory's correctional facility. The task of shortening the period of purification and obtaining parole before the eternal bliss of paradise is one that has become highly associated with the month of November as surviving relatives are most anxious to see their loved ones sprung from any place of temporary torment. The practice of prayer, having masses said and indulgences offered is one that has become central to many of the Catholic faith during November. As ever, younger folk, keen as always to redefine themselves, have interpreted Purgatory in a different way and use the term 'love purgatory' to refer to a libidinous limbo-land when one experiences the absolute tragedy of meeting the love of one's life at the wrong time. However, with just three months to go to Valentines' Day and with lots of Christmas liquor to be consumed, November prayers of the younger generation, while ignoring the spiritual fate of their forefathers, may lead to a yielding of the heavenly gates of romance sooner than anticipated.

No November would be complete without reference to the great American tradition of Thanksgiving. While Thanksgiving is a day when we pause to give thanks for the things we have, Remembrance Day is a day we pause to give thanks to the people who fought for the things we have.

World Pneumonia Day

The 12 November every year has been assigned as the day when would-be patients of the planet demand action from those responsible for global health policy in the fight against pneumonia. This potentially deadly infection is, after all, preventable and treatable with vaccines, antibiotics and improved sanitation, yet it annually claims the lives of millions of children and vulnerable adults around the world. For those who are terrorised by the thought of anyone with a sniffle even looking in their direction, significant anxiety is generated by the notion of a potentially transmissible illness such as pneumonia. Yet it was relatively recently that medical professionals were acknowledging the bad news that a cure for the common cold remained elusive while celebrating the good news that pneumonia was in fact treatable, with antibiotics being the veritable silver bullet for this once deadly infection. Over time, this led to a certain complacency about this hitherto slayer of the meek and less robust, and it wasn't just the 'p' in pneumonia that was silent as medics and their patients lowered their guard against this previously virulent but now tameable bug. With all-conquering medicines and the memory of this illness fading, you could almost be forgiven for wondering if bronchopneumonia was a condition affecting horses as opposed to their riders.

In the past, pneumonia was regarded as the harbinger of a ghastly doom with drenching fevers and delirium the calling card of the grim reaper. Many a yesteryear medic who diagnosed pneumonia in the less-affluent communities was surprised to be thanked for making the diagnosis as the hapless victims would have their rations halved so the food wasn't wasted. In the past, people frequently expressed a bizarre gratitude for contracting this respiratory ailment when writhing on their deathbed as pneumonia was often the final complication of many illnesses and often a merciful release. Pneumonia, like tuberculosis, didn't just seem to run in deprived families and communities, it seemed to take its time to get to know each one of them personally. Pneumonia was seen as a perverse Christmas gift for those lacking shelter or sustenance during the raw chill of winter as it invariably signalled that suffering and deprivation would soon be over. The sense of doom induced by this contagion was temporarily mitigated at the start of the antibiotic era when antibiotics changed the perception of one's fate as soon as spiking temperatures made their appearance.

Antibiotics were initially perceived as proof that God did not want us to suffer. Science demonstrated, through miraculous invention, that even if life layered our bread with mould, we could always make penicillin. Pneumonia was no longer seen as the final reckoning but came to be perceived as an event that afforded the sufferer a duvet day with the remote control to hand while having to swallow a few oversized capsules. Moral judgement was quick to creep in, however, as seasoned health professionals assumed the patient's respiratory ills were as a result of nicotine addiction rather than pneumonia. The shame and stigma of self-inflicted wounds and burdened health services lead to many warnings as the link between smoking and respiratory infection was established. It certainly took the fun out of attending emergency departments as primarily older smokers were subjected to an unparalleled level of human intimacy, if not interrogation, as swabs were aggressively rotated in nostrils in the quest for tracing adaptable respiratory pathogens. If pneumonia bugs took on different forms in the past, they could be neutralised with ever-more effective antibiotics. Even the most deadly aspiration pneumonia could be dismissed as a condition of social climbers.

So how did it all go so wrong? It seems that those younger scientists forgot the most fundamental law of nature (and microbiology) when applied to antibiotics: the drugs that fail to kill bugs invariably make those bugs stronger. There is little doubt that bacterial resistance to antibiotics now threatens to reverse decades of medical progress in treating illnesses such as pneumonia. The folly of allowing antibiotics into the human food chain and allowing farmers to (over)use them for their livestock now seems to be sinking in. Had those younger experts never heard of time-honoured virtues such as providence and prudence, if not sensible, rational science, when it came to using valuable resources?

What advice do I give to those most vulnerable to airway pestilence? There seems little for older people to do during periods of peak influenza other than take sensible precautions such as availing of the flu vaccine before the onset of the sniffle season. Additionally, although it may seem a tad antisocial, asking grandchildren and carers not to visit if they have symptoms of respiratory infection may be the only way to protect those who are vulnerable to pneumonia. An ounce of prevention is worth a pound of cure, and a period of self-imposed isolation may be the only way to avoid needing the two or three courses of antibiotics necessary to quell the more virulent strains of the pneumonia bug. At the end of their lives, few older people will bemoan having taken time off work to replenish and turbo-charge the immune system. After all, nobody on their deathbed should wish that they spent more time in the office … unless they left the office early and got caught in a shower that resulted in a chill, developed into pneumonia and led to their untimely demise!

Cyber Monday

You could be forgiven for thinking the term 'Cyber Monday' referred to an Orwellian phenomenon of a space invasion, sneakily set for the start of the working week to catch the human race off guard. It actually refers to the marketing term who work for the Monday after Thanksgiving in the United States and was deliberately (and literally) coined to persuade people to shop online. The phrase was devised by Ellen Davis of the National Retail Foundation in America. It was first used within the commerce community during the 2005 holiday season to officially kick off the online retail spending spree in the lead-up to Christmas. For older shoppers who like a bargain but are terrorised by the prospect of Black Friday's hungry hordes of consumers and who would prefer to engage in non-violent holiday shopping, the Monday after Black Friday should have an instinctive appeal. The rushing crowds, the fear of being trampled, the risk of pepper-spraying and the long queues during Black Friday, Cyber Monday seems the perfect Black Friday equivalent for the older introverts and the safety obsessed. Admittedly, after years of Monday-morning lassitude, older retirees may have little practice in the art of appearing focused at the start of the week. Cyber Monday, therefore, may catch even the savviest shopper off guard when it comes to looking forward to Monday in any way. With 'Remorse Tuesday' and 'Hiding from Creditors Wednesday', there is always a financial downside to punish those on a fixed income who yield to impulse purchases from the privacy of one's abode.

For those who braved the mob on Black Friday and whose injuries were not severe enough to prevent them clicking a mouse a few days later, window shopping may be the perfect foreplay for those who resisted everything, including temptation. In fact, if older people listen closely enough, they will be able to hear Cyber Monday sharpening its claws and licking its virtual lips as the older consumer finally sheds their inhibitions and gets ready to buy what they like as opposed to what they need. Having first established that Cyber Monday has nothing to do with sex messaging, it begins to look a lot like Christmas for those in search of a holiday bargain whilst aiming to stretch the value of their Bitcoinage. Many older shoppers log on in the hope of saving hard currency but should be aware they may be inadvertently perpetuating a stereotype that all older people are mean and simply want to avoid parking charges at the local shopping centre. The joy of finding that most retailers offer free shipping of their products to their desired destination may add to the parsimonious reputation of older people, but this does not mean products have to cross the high seas as the term implies, hence somewhat muting the joy of bargain-hunting. The free shipping concession does make shopping a lot more convenient for older people nonetheless. It is a lot more convenient than going to a retailer's brick and mortar store. Other savvy senior spenders will know, however, that the term 'Cyber Monday' exists for the benefit of retailers only and that an extended post-Thanksgiving sale is usually a daily event anyway in the run up to Christmas.

Actual navigation of the shopping frenzy on the day requires a deftness of hand and ultra-rapid reflexes to click at the right time to avoid the crashing of sites, the selling out of coveted items and the rapid depletion of one's personal account, not to mention clicking on the wrong item, size or colour of the object of one's attention. The surge of happiness and anticipation on locating the top item on the shopping list with a major markdown may, in true rollercoaster fashion, be followed by desperation as the site crashes just as said item has been added to the shopping cart. Not only is the whole exercise a job for the bifocals but also for one's conscience as the superego continues to ask awkward questions and prompt ever-more internal debate as to the necessity of the item. Having overcome intense inner scepticism and guilt and parted with hard-earned savings or most of one's fixed weekly income, the computer log-out is inevitably accompanied by a nauseated, elated feeling mixed with anxiety that leaves one shamefully scrambling for the contact details of local addiction services. If each day is a gift as one gets older, a day of internet shopping on Cyber Monday threatens to pose questions about the returns policy regarding Mondays themselves, and not just in relation to the actual items purchased. A sense of black humour can buffer some of Cyber Monday's frustrations, however, as older people gleefully remind themselves that with any gift for others, it is always the thought that counts more than the shockingly little amount that was spent on it.

What underpins events such as Cyber Monday is the reality that the internet and its marketplace are not the exclusive domain of younger people; older people have enthusiastically adopted most, if not all, online activities. When the internet was developed during the 1990s, older people, otherwise known as silver surfers, became avid and consistent users of this new technology. Whilst there have been concerns that the rise in internet usage among the younger population has led to fears of isolation, the increase in the use of the medium for older people has had the opposite effect. Rates of clinical depression for older people may even be reduced by as much as 20 to 28 percent with greater internet usage, according to research conducted by Cotten et al. at the University of Alabama. As ever, with age comes certain qualities that should be kept in mind in relation to the internet; these include reason, balance, life knowledge and a healthy degree of scepticism that is only possessed by cunning seniors, attributes which can never be discounted or sold during Cyber Monday. That entire package only comes via an online dating site where older people, along with the occasional aid of Photoshop, can successfully market themselves on a daily basis, and not just on Cyber Monday!

DECEMBER

Advent – Let's Prepare

The cynical, reluctant, pre-yuletide reveller will tell you that Christmas has lost its meaning as they stagger with incumbent hangover from one office party to another. The older advent adventurer will quietly observe that it is not Christmas itself that has become destitute of worth and value, but the three to four weeks of advent, which is the prelude to the main event of Christmas Day. As people grow older and receive the gift of maturation and wisdom to cure themselves of many youthful follies, they undoubtedly question the obsession with the two-month shopping festival that culminates in one extremely large roast meal on a cold December day. Just how much shopping can a body do for a single repast? Advent was originally intended to be a season of fasting, much like Lent, in anticipation of the celebration of the nativity of Jesus at Christmas. Yet, fasting and self-restraint is the last thing on people's minds. The term 'advent' is a version of the Latin word meaning 'coming'. Far from expectant waiting and soulful preparation, the advent wreath can quickly become advent wrath as expectations grow and fuses shorten amidst the flurry that is the run up to Christmas. What strategies do older people need to stay cool during yule?

In my view, the emotional juggernaut that is Christmas should be seen as a looming personal crisis that requires intervention from a multi-agency crisis-response team. The equivalent to this in one's own brain is to coordinate and mobilise as many calming neural pathways as possible to shield against Christmas calamities. In many ways, the month of December is a victim of and complete hostage to the dominatrix that is Christmas. This same dominatrix insists on holding a compulsory party where all sorts of dopamine-inducing behaviours get flaunted like a cocaine dealer selling their illicit wares to prepare for the said carouse. Although the drug of choice for many seniors is a cosy chair in front of an uninterrupted TV, other elders are less than immune to the giddy excitement of the Christmas build-up. The behaviours displayed include frenzied shopping, reckless spending, imbibing to vast extremes, round-the-clock socialising and a sense of deadline completion as if the planet was destined to end. Gone is the potential for a quiet, mellow, serotonin-induced reflection at year's end as many a wary older Christmas sceptic gets sucked into the vile vortex of consumerism. The advent antidote must be to step back to a place of considered reflection and plan, at an early stage, a non-participation or at least a damage-limitation strategy for the unfolding Christmas lunacy. What are the ingredients for a more reticent repose during December?

The curse of perfectionism seems to stalk most, if not all, of us during advent, affecting every behaviour and attitude, which we outwardly or inwardly express during the Christmas sprint. We need to challenge the notion that any Christmas gift that we purchase wrapped up in tinsel and brightly coloured paper will transform anyone's life. As with any gift, to borrow if not to purchase the well-worn cliché, it is the thought that counts and irrespective of the price tag, it should be patently obvious that the expression of love contained in a gift is better than anything we can wrap. Although most people do their best to brighten their abode before the big day, we need to overcome the familiar disappointment that we haven't succeeded in transforming our homes into a fairytale St. Anton ski chalet. Our self-maintenance tasks such as attending to hair, teeth and nails can wait until the new year – as can the new bathroom, new sofa and redecorating. Canny older consumers know all too well that whilst businesses pull the shutters down for a few days over Christmas, all are compelled to reopen by the new year. For example, hair needs to be cut, permed and dyed during the rest of the year. Making our Christmas Day expectations realistic as opposed to fantastical is the key to managing the inevitable disappointments for which we set ourselves up during advent. This includes a healthy but not cynical scepticism regarding the enhanced levels of familial devotion that we are suddenly supposed to display, even if parents and their offspring haven't been on speaking terms since last Christmas.

Declan Lyons

Avoiding over-preparation for Christmas is vital if we are to avoid succumbing to OCD (Obsessive Christmas Disorder), the signs of which may have become well established during advent. Older cooks who zealously, faithfully and perennially prepare Christmas fare such as cakes or puddings for their offspring, neighbours and friends may find their entire efforts are in vain if their gourmet produce is recycled as puppy treats because tastes have moved on from marzipan covered in sugar. In terms of such mass production, Christmas cooks would do well to exercise the kind of restraint that prevents them from consuming a chocolate advent calendar all in one go. Preparation for all the demands of Christmas has its uses but also its limits; the world will still revolve on its axis even if we miss the date for posting abroad or forget to send a card or two, even if the cards arrive so late as to be out of season and are smudged by the suntan lotion on the postman's hands. Equally, being selective and discerning about social invitations that are both issued and accepted during advent may help maintain precious energy levels for the main event. On the other hand, running one's immune system ragged and contracting a virus on Christmas Day may absolve one from participation in the domestic slavery that sees one's cooking facilities working overtime.

Sometimes advent can be a metaphor for life itself as we aim to pace ourselves ahead of the main event by keeping reserves in the tank and avoiding the over-hyping of what is, after all, just one day. It is necessary to check our assumptions as we serially drift into cosy catastrophe, year-in, year-out, whilst trying to raise the bar on last year's offerings. It may be time for an older generation to partially mobilise their inner scrooge or at least some attributes of self-defence in order to stay the course during this most frantic of times. By making Christmas sustainable for all and successfully overseeing the season of bonhomie, elders can be role models for the young in managing the rest of the year.

The Twelve Challenges of Christmas

Christmas is a time of strong emotions and high expectations, a time to reflect on lost loved ones and a time to survive and hopefully recover from the stress of shopping, spending and preparing for seasonal parties and gatherings. In childhood, time seemed to stretch into the infinite future and Christmases were separated by an eternity, but as we grow older, most people feel a distinct acceleration in the passage of time. Last year's decorations have barely hit the attic when it's time to extract them once again and check how many have survived removal from the human gaze in the recesses of our storage space. We may even notice that we still have traces of last year's Christmas tree in our car boot or behind the sofa. These observations, which become increasingly apparent in our later years, may reinforce the view that Christmas is essentially about implanting happy memories into children before they grow up to realise how not-so-great life can be. Ignoring the health warnings and reality checks that come by holding up and gazing into the yuletide mirror, can older people retrieve a meaningful connection with the festive season, and if so, what strategies do they require to achieve this?

Recognise that it will soon be upon us. However ambivalent we may be, however we long for a diversion from screaming grandchildren, Christmas is happening and preparations 'to seize the season' are required to avoid a loss of momentum. After all, Christmas melts the misery of a long, dark winter, and what better antidote to the winter blues than a splash of sparkle and colour in advance of spring?

As we prepare for the twelve-day shutdown, a sense of **positive pessimism** may be prudent, as well as being armed with the latest weather predictions from postmen in Donegal and New

Zealand. It being mid-winter, we may face meteorological hazards in the form of snow and ice, hence having stocked up on tins and extra provisions to ensure the essentials are well covered is vital. Giving some thought to ordering medication from your pharmacy well in advance of Christmas Eve is also an idea. Having your boiler serviced before winter's onset may seem fatalistic but is infinitely better than leaving innumerable voice messages for emergency repair services that turn out to be less contactable than their *Golden Pages* ad suggests.

Compiling a **Christmas diary** or list of essential tasks may be very helpful in shifting us into forward gear when we have finally acknowledged the imminence of the season. How many cards do we send this year? Do we want to write our phone numbers after our signature or include a more personal greeting to invite further contact throughout the year, which may be useful in dispelling moments of isolation when the twelve days of Christmas are behind us? Apart from purchasing exorbitantly priced gifts for our loved ones, who do we really want to thank for their support to us throughout the year? That pharmacist perhaps?

Well-aimed gifts, received or donated, can make or break a season which has become dominated by all things commercial. When giving to significant others, be sure to judge the gift according to the person's tastes or interests without imposing your own. Enclosing a gift receipt can allow the recipient to redeem the more risky purchases. Gift tokens are perfectly acceptable nowadays and online shopping can remove the hassle factor as well as saving time and money. Do remember to clear the internet search history if you're using your son's or daughter's device to purchase their gift!

Consider writing a **list of tasks** that will definitely, positively, absolutely be **postponed** until the new year. This will not only fill the empty diary when our personal trainer or physiotherapist is more available but will avoid the unnecessary stress we impose on ourselves to get everything done in that final, Armageddon-like week before Christmas.

Set a **tone of openness** by having frank discussions with those close to us about our personal expectations and practical arrangements for Christmas. This can include gift preferences for something essential such as a fuel voucher, assistance with putting up the decorations or even dinner or transport arrangements during the season. Personal care may also be hard to come by during the twelve days when many support services shut down; organising a family rota is prudent in these circumstances.

When the day arrives, **enter into the spirit** of the season by participating in festive rituals, religious services and Christmas events. This is the time to let go of the stress of recent weeks and recover the true essence of past Christmases, as well as spontaneously giving and receiving words and deeds of festive cheer.

For those suffering through a recent **bereavement**, Christmas may seem like an emotional rollercoaster, a day to be simply endured. It is important to acknowledge the loss, to talk about the deceased person, to share memories and even do something that would have made your loved one smile. Lighting a candle will honour their memory and illuminate the void that has been left behind but also connect us with a poignant past and a spiritual future as we end the year.

Communicating with loved ones is the essence of Christmas and new technology may make this easier, especially for those living overseas. Complacency and a tendency to make less effort to have actual face-to-face contact should be avoided, however, as many older people may see a text message as a poor substitute for a heart-to-heart on the phone. Above all, most older people dislike the stereotyped view of old age as being equated with loneliness and isolation or a need for charity. Christmas communication should thus be more than just a time-consuming duty or a necessary therapy for adult children to enact. It should be a prelude to the regular bonding between generations throughout the year.

Food, and the variety and quantity of it, is the substance that binds if not constipates people of all ages during the festivities. Food preparation requires military precision in its planning, timing and delivery to avoid the excesses of hunger and over-indulgence. Succumbing to intoxication can obliterate efforts to bite tongues, utter niceties and generally be diplomatic during what may seem a long, drawn-out culinary incarceration. Exercise, water and the well-timed and socially acceptable nap can offset most of the associated excesses.

Consider if circumstances allow **changing your Christmas routine** and traditions. How about going away for Christmas, having your dinner in a different venue, having a meal with neighbours or opting for a vegetarian or alternative menu? It's never too late to construct a new narrative, diversion or theme for this time of year, and your spring social life may blossom in the process.

The best **Christmas virtues** to cultivate and put into practice include enthusiasm, humour and a sense of supreme patience. Although some may perceive the departure from routine as a burden and others may have impossibly high expectations of this time of year, it is above all a time to count blessings and indulge in a little nostalgia as we remind ourselves that we should reflect on the many relationships that we have enjoyed and continue to enjoy and how they can be nurtured in the years we have left.

Christmas carries many obligations and demands which, with a little pre-planning, can be more easily borne and even enjoyed. Those in the rat race of the working life have the chance to slow down for a week or two, but even for those who have long-vacated that frenzied groove, in a world which is hell-bent on doing, the Christmas season offers a pleasant opportunity for being.

Surviving Toxic Relatives at Yuletide

At Christmas, almost all roads lead home (unless you happen to be on permanent duty as an emergency services employee) and the proverbial spotlight is ritually shone on the family network, as custom compels us to be in close proximity for a period of time with those who share more than a shred of our DNA. The cynical older yuletide reveller may frequently proclaim that Christmas is just for children whilst branding the festive season as a chore, a headache and a nightmare, hence cutting out the work for a younger generation who have the task of defrosting their chilled hearts. As multiple generations gather together, what sanity-saving strategies does one need to adopt to get through those not-so-silent nights with the next of kin? Staying merry and bright may be easier for those who enthuse over the perfect present, yet it takes an older person to appreciate that the best gift of all is the presence of a happy family all wrapped up in each other. In reality, family life can be the bane or meaning of one's existence. Nowadays, finding a blissful gathering modelled on the original of 2,000 years ago in a town named Bethlehem in the Middle East may prove somewhat challenging; the proverbial prickly holly rather than soft tinsel is more likely to be exchanged, especially as the days' festivities degenerate into recrimination over conflicts nearly as old as the Christmas manger itself. The comedian George Burns noted: 'Happiness is having a large, loving, caring, close-knit family in another city'. In reality, such a metropolis may be an unattainable, albeit heavenly place as the homing instinct grows stronger and harder to resist at Christmas.

Older people may retain hard-wired memories of Christmas when they themselves were expectant children hanging onto Santa's every whim and delighting in simple treats in that bygone era of simplicity and innocence. Marriage subsequently gave them an opportunity to inherit an additional dysfunctional family, just in case the one they originated from wasn't enough. By then, they were in the driving seat when it came to coming home for Christmas and often made enormous sacrifices to ensure the festival was extra special for their offspring. The proverbial serpents' sharp tooth of ingratitude from those flushed with youth, however, along with that generation's higher and higher expectations of the season and life in general, threatened to undermine the functioning of increasingly dysfunctional families during the holiday season. This could leave an older generation walking on eggshells rather than sunshine when the kids stopped by over Christmas as historical conflicts and frustrations would be ritually aired.

No matter what level of restraint is practised by parents in my therapy room, fifteen minutes into the festive season, they become hopelessly enmeshed in those old dynamics with their kids. I believe it is truly ironic that older people are in therapy to learn how to deal with people who should be in therapy themselves. It's not that the spoiled-brat generation wouldn't like to be on the therapist's couch – just don't ask them to pay for it; as so-called dysfunctional family survivors they truly believe that's what Mom and Dad are for. The nub of the problem, as I have observed as the gatekeeper of the said couch, seems to be the barrel over which the old can be held by the young. If parents opt out of the holiday outing, the end result may be a prolonged guilt-trip or a long unwanted trip with no contact with their children or grandchildren. Older people can be especially sensitive to a state of isolation and loneliness, and the feeling of being unwanted is the most terrible poverty at Christmas or indeed at any other time of year. If there truly is no option but to endure rather than effect a cure, then the advice of George Bernard Shaw may be particularly apt when he said 'If you cannot get rid of the family skeleton, you may as well make it dance'.

Changing dynamics and keeping the peace during the festive season means giving up on the perpetual expectation that familiar visitors to our homes will improve their conduct. It's most unlikely that offspring who are playing the roles of tyrant, bully, drama queen or victim will suddenly morph into a more mature, considerate version of themselves. If 'toddler on the verge of meltdown' impersonations are a personal forte, then expect more renditions and try to accept this as a cry for love and recognition. Nonetheless, a secure boundary setting as to what or who will be tolerated should be seriously planned. How can the toxic influence of the insufferable relative be mitigated? Do you have an exit plan? How much time can you really endure in their company without wishing for an acute choking attack or other medical emergency that might mercifully intervene? Perhaps if an A&E visit seems preferable to sharing a turkey carcass with kinsfolk, then the wisdom of their or your invitation to partake in the festivities should be questioned.

Halting the need to control the actions of our offspring can be extremely difficult but potentially transformative. If we perpetually slip into that critical-parent mode around our progeny, should we really be surprised when they regress to a childlike state around us? Accepting full responsibility for our part in laying down a new dynamic of dialogue and respect is likely to be much more fruitful. Becoming a sage-like observer of the participants around the Christmas table is likely to lead to greater psychological awareness of them and ourselves in terms of behaviours we recognise that facilitate other people's dysfunctional ways. Changing a dynamic that previously seemed set in stone and require us to tiptoe around in order to preserve a fragile harmony can have big effects. Having a good debrief that is laden with laughter and that acknowledges our efforts at family diplomacy is also a vital part of navigating the Christmas stage and the actors that strode onto it. Roll on next year!

New Year's: Resolutions/Revolutions Yet Again

As Christmas slips away and the central heating saps the life out of the Christmas tree, the arrival of year's end tempts us to gear up for another bloated hangover as we prepare to ring in the start of another year. There is absolutely no arguing with the calendar – another year has arrived, and we must face the consequences of clocking up an ever-greater mileage on life's clock. It's not that a single increment of our chronological score is threatening it itself – it is more the accumulated effect, like the inflation-driven total of all those perennial increases in rail fare that threatens our end-of-year psychological balance sheet. However eagerly or reluctantly we embrace the new year, we should allow ourselves a mini-victory or two that may temporarily blunt the scythe of the grim reaper. We have survived Christmas, after all: we prevented the occurrence of acute gout or alcoholic hepatitis from over-indulgence, we circumvented toxic constipation, avoided the Heimlich manoeuvre to retrieve un-masticated turkey chunks and avoided the treacherous fall over the Christmas tree. These are no mean achievements during a season of apparent goodwill. What better motivation is there to reassess, take stock and clean the slate for a fresh listing of life's priorities than an unscathed emergence from a period of debauchery? For older people who may already head-shakingly disapprove of seasonal intemperance, is there anything to be gained or (more likely) lost by brainstorming a new year's resolution or two, or should older dogs be left to sleep without being expected to learn new tricks?

Older people may seem to have natural advantages when it comes to the new year and turning over a new leaf. The greatest labour-saving device available to the human race is procrastination, which means things that should be prudently tackled today can be stealthily brushed aside until tomorrow. Because of retirement and an abundance of time on our hands, various types of distraction can feed into a perennial struggle for self-control. It's ironic that those who should be most flooded with apprehension at the passing of time can be most cavalier about this same dimension when freed from its worst strictures. Missing the burst of expectation that ought to launch the new year, however, may seem to some to be a missed opportunity. Setting our intention on the crest of a wave of enthusiasm is a vital ingredient for some in shaking mothballs from dreams and visualising change. When we were young, the new year was a vast landscape ripe for cultivation, but as we accumulate years, new year's resolutions driven purely by vanity are likely to result in self-reproach, disappointment and higher Botox bills.

Having already survived a haze of multiple indulgences, older people may be cynical about the value of restraint and abstinence when it comes to the old dependables that are grist to the resolution mill: smoking, drinking and physical inactivity. They shrewdly know that those who exercise most in their jobs, such as on-foot postmen, aren't immortal, while that creature that rarely moves at all lives longest, namely the tortoise. Do seasoned but serially failed resolutionaries who have survived if not thrived by letting their hair down (along with more than a few beers, excess carbohydrates and cigar smoke) during their lifetime now really need to adopt a Ghandi-like asceticism and simply pass up on life's few pleasures and indulgences? Are new year's resolutions an opportunity to not only take responsibility for ourselves, but to also dream with our eyes open? Resolutions that are dreamed up under the influence of alcohol are likely to be fickle, especially if we can't remember them the next day.

Some people take resolutions seriously whilst others bid farewell to good intentions just after the clock strikes twelve. It is estimated that fewer than 10 percent of people manage to keep their resolutions for more than a few months. It is generally the privations such as losing weight and quitting smoking that are betrayed right away. This has the potential to remind us of a sense of failure all year round if that expanding abdomen is perpetually incompatible with one's self-image. If you've built up a backlog of underachievement over a lifetime with a limited number of years ahead to make amends, it is important not to revisit failed resolutions. Whilst this may sound like a depressing admission of failure, it can be quite liberating to never have to join a Weight Watchers group again or buy nicotine-replacement patches. Being realistic about any resolution is crucial too. How likely is it that we will become an accomplished cellist within one year or write a book and sell the film rights within twelve months? Considering a mid-January reset-day if your resolution falls by the wayside at the first hurdle rather than abandoning the cause entirely when an old friend drops unexpectedly by and those extra-calorie treats just beg to be served. A two-year resolution accommodates longer-term aspirations such as being elected to political office and high-risk, seemingly preposterous goals such as learning to ski downhill, para-glide or scuba-dive. We should never forget that new year resolutions also incorporate deeply pragmatic goals such as learning to be more compliant, practicing meditation, paying greater attention to our health, expanding social networks beyond the active retirement group, watching less TV or even letting go of grudges before they're etched on our tombstone.

It could be argued that later life is the perfect time to make truly balanced resolutions as we renew life's contract with ourselves as opposed to the whims or demands of the wider society. How refreshing is it that when new year rolls by annually, we are always provided with the opportunity to dust off neglected talents, mix up our routine and leave room for the unplanned, the unpredictable and the downright astonishing? We may decide to become creative, express ourselves artistically, learn a new skill or even resolve personal baggage. Though our bodies seem to be falling apart at times, it is never too late to finally get our heads together.

THE DAYS OF THE WEEK THROUGH OLDER EYES

Magical Mondays

For those who bemoaned spending one seventh of their entire lives inhabiting the bleak territory that was all those serial Mondays, yet who were brave or idiotic enough to repeatedly turn up for the start of more working weeks, one of the consequences of retirement is that Monday and all its associations may decidedly feel more optional than compulsory. The resentment of having a weekend of happiness interrupted by Mondays, only to have scheduled joy resume briefly on a Friday, has always tormented those who occupy multiple roles such as worker, commuter, family provider or anyone who has adhered to a basic weekly schedule. The torture of locating Monday so far away from Friday and positioning Friday so close to Monday seems a deliberate tease to the leisure worshipper who craves endless weekends. As work demands more and more of our time and headspace, increasingly threatening to convert carefree hedonists into crazed workaholics, there is less and less time to do even the washing-up, let alone pursue our dreams. If leisure is your treasure then retirement can open up many new horizons with an expanse of free time to do activities ranging from the fairly standard to the entirely unconventional. That secret saxophonist, butterfly collector, falconer or beach nudist lurking for years under a cloak of mediocrity and convention may finally emerge once that dreaded weekday which is Monday takes on an entirely different meaning.

The name of Monday is derived from Old and Middle English and literally means 'moon day'. Naming Earth's only permanent natural satellite after the least popular day of the week seems to do a disservice to a planet that has beguiled and fascinated humanity long before space travel and Apollo missions were possible. The gravitational pull of the moon is said to produce ocean and body tides to which some attribute higher rates of insanity in susceptible individuals, and likewise, Mondays can be said to exert a similar force on human beings, being associated with a higher rate of depression, sick days and other absences from work. Many popular songs feature Monday as a day of depression, anxiety or melancholy such as 'I Don't Like Mondays' from the Boomtown Rats (1979) or 'Manic Monday' from the Bangles (1986). Even if it has been predetermined by the average employee that a day off on Monday is long overdue for whatever reason, be it an anticipated hangover, good weather or a birthday, the day itself may be more than tinged with discomfort as the would-be escapee has to pull off a convincing 'sickie' and make that uncomfortable call notifying a more-often-than-not skeptical boss about their fake symptoms. The value of the said 'sickie' must surely be also questionable if it means having to avoid all shops for the day to prevent bumping into one's boss out on an impromptu lunchtime-spending-spree. Whilst bank holidays may seem to offer respite from the weekly misery of Monday, they are in reality few and far between and are promptly followed by Tuesday, which may be considered the ugly sister of Monday, being a vast four days from the start of the weekend. Given the weekly battering to the spirit administered every Monday to those of working age, it is not hard to see why even the perpetually optimistic, who see each day as a gift, would gladly return Mondays.

Older people in grateful and voluntary exile from the rat race who are seasoned linguists will know, however, that Monday contains *mon* or 'mine' in French, helping them realise that Monday can in fact be thought of as 'my day', which is an altogether much more promising note by which to begin the week. Gone is the obligatory start to the weekly diet, the shedding of the pyjamas for the pantyhose or pinstripe, or the anticipation of a new Friday arriving in four days, which seems like an eternity away. In fact, the simple awareness that one no longer has to ritually mourn the ending of the weekend on Mondays and that the weekend newspapers can be digested in a leisurely fashion and coffee slowly sipped seems like early parole to the recalcitrant offender. Shifting that sinking Sunday epigastric sensation and savouring the freedom may take some time for retirees, however, as their brains have been programmed to expect obligations to recommence on Mondays since they first entered full-time education at (on average) 5 years of age. We can also be forgiven for failing to immediately shed that dazed, newly released prisoner look as we slowly realise that we don't have to confine our trademark blowout behaviours such as alcohol or other indulgences to the early part of the weekend. It can be greatly revitalising to realise that if we have a reasonable baseline level of health and vigour, we can start the week with high energy and not expect it to peter out during the week when everyone other than us gets to benefit from our toils. Mondays can be the start of new and fresh beginnings as we turn our preconceptions on their collective heads to seize opportunities and to get more done, rather than scrambling to get all the postponed business of the week and the chores of living completed by 5 pm on Saturday. We may even find we have that coveted restaurant table all to ourselves on Mondays to eat healthily as we jettison all those bad habits that resurfaced over the weekend.

If the days of the week are a sort of microcosm of life itself, then older people could be said to be living out of weekend days, whereas the young start their lives on Monday and reach middle age by Wednesday or Thursday. The gift of post-retirement Monday is that everyone can start afresh, irrespective of age, without having to claw at the remnants of the weekend just passed or berating themselves for how little they have achieved during that forty-eight-hour window. Swapping the weekend and weekday lenses for just a single pair can help magnify the optimism, potential and opportunity that a week-start rather than a week-end can bring. This insight is thankfully available to all, but the conversion from Monday survivor to Monday admirer, and the freedom to break the patterns of a lifetime, comes eventually to those who wait.

THE HAPPIEST HUMP DAYS

No matter how often we resolve not to start our day with the broken pieces of yesterday and resolve to remind ourselves that today is the first day of the rest of our lives, it is hard not to remember all the things that weren't accomplished on Monday or the guilt we will feel if we postpone them until Wednesday or later. If the first five days of the week are the hardest, then at least by Tuesday the shock of the start of the week has abated slightly. If Sunday and Monday are about renewal, then Tuesday, Wednesday and Thursday are about the business of living. Older survivors of the daily and weekly grind may be cynical and ungracious about Tuesday, seeing it as a random chunk of 24 hours with nothing going for it, although if Tuesday could speak, it would surely defend itself by denying any relationship with Monday.

Veterans of serial lots of seven consecutive days may sense that Wednesday, albeit a middle day, heralds the start of looking forward to things to come. For many wading through Wednesday, Thursday may represent the real start to the weekend, with only one day to go until Friday. As latter-day masters of their destiny and leisure, older people, bolstered by wisdom, may become sceptical about the merits of perpetually waiting for Fridays, or for summertime and holidays, or for someone to fall in love with them. Does this confer a reality-check advantage on seasoned life voyagers who can (and actually must!) really live in the moment and not wish their lives away? Or, should older people simply put their heads down during the week and get in shape to light the weekend fireworks? Americans, who kick off the four-yearly eviction and re-tenancy of the occupant of 1600 Pennsylvania Avenue, Washington DC, get to display their approval or otherwise of the would-be incumbents and their electability, on Super Tuesday in either February or March of the presidential election year. This is the day when the greatest number of states hold primary elections and caucuses, and the greatest number of delegates to the summer's presidential nominating conventions can be won by either party on Super Tuesday. The sheer responsibility of such a momentous decision being serially thrust on the shoulders of just any old day would be too much for frivolous Friday or moody Monday, so Tuesday, when weekend hangovers have been safely dispersed, has been wisely conscripted for the task.

For the politically naive who assume Super Tuesday is similar to Black Friday and who head to shopping malls seeking discounts at 3 am, this auspicious day could turn out to be a disappointing second Monday instead of a sink-or-swim boot camp for ambitious political campaigns. For Tuesday thrift seekers, all may not be lost, however, as a range of discounts may be on offer as older people may avail of a range of discounted goods and services, from cheap cinema tickets to restaurants and cut-price apparel. The absence of the hordes makes for a double perk, as seniors may have those coveted changing rooms all to themselves whilst leisurely inhaling waistlines as they squeeze into garments on Tuesdays, Wednesdays and Thursdays, when the real business of their week can get done.

By Wednesday, with half the working week over, some seniors may fondly recall the traditional half day that workers and school students availed of as many businesses, institutions and even high street shops closed their collective doors – a tradition that now seems as curiously charming as returning home to eat one's main meal in the middle of the day, as we live in an ever more homogenised, commerce-obsessed and fast-paced world. Perhaps the reason for the nursery rhyme describing Wednesday's child as being full of woe was the gradual theft of the beloved half day by the corporate clique. In America, Wednesday became known as 'Hump Day' from the 1960's onwards, alluding to the fact that Wednesday is the middle of the week, meaning that one has made it 'over the hump' and toward the weekend. (It was not an ageist reference to spinal curvature in older people or a celebration of the virtues of the camel as a means of transport in the desert.) Some will acknowledge Wednesday as potentially the toughest day of the week with Thursday unofficially launching the weekend, but Wednesday metaphorically implies a climb up a proverbial hill to get through a hard and challenging week.

Adopting an astrological perspective to the weekdays and their meaning is to align ourselves with the planetary attributes and work with the cosmic orbits, as opposed to blindly stumbling through the week. Tuesday is therefore said to be influenced by the aggression of Mars, the Greek god of war, and is therefore associated with effectiveness and the completion of tasks. Why step on Friday's drunken toes, after all? Wednesday, being ruled by Mercury, the messenger of the heavens, facilitates clear communication and synchronicity. In many ways Wednesday is a vital link to all other days and is akin to the network server of the week. For older people who are shy with technology, this can still be an excellent day to correspond, quill in hand, using the leisurely mail of the snails. Thursday is all about business and productivity, being associated with Jupiter, the planet of enterprise and expansion. Being a day of smooth deceleration toward the weekend implies quickening the pace of networking, socialising and marketing. If one is thinking of investing pension funds or backing a start-up, for example, then Thursday may be the shrewdest day to invoke planetary approbation.

Midweek days may seem like occasions to sit extremely still to avoid being seen by the dreaded Tuesdays, Wednesdays or Thursdays. While creativity and ambition may have slumped as we struggled with mid-week blues in the past, reaching retirement age allows us time and space to jump-start our genius and imagination as we seize all the opportunities, ranging from mid-week breaks to mid-week madness.

FRIVOLOUS, FLIGHTY FRIDAYS

Getting up on a Friday morning and enthusiastically saying hello to the world's favourite day of the week is a behaviour that would be well-nigh impossible on any other weekday, particularly those that are notoriously and collectively despised such as Monday. In fact, if Friday was a person, although it is regularly abandoned for six other days of the week, it would be consoled by the knowledge that those who passed through Monday to Thursday were really thinking of it the whole time and had remained zealous, enthusiastic and even obsessive Friday-fans throughout. If Friday had a face it would be kissed to the point of blistering as the world lines up to let its collective hair down and welcomes the weekend. That Friday feeling and the feeling of sheer abandonment as work is left behind for the weekend, a two-day cease-fire in the midst of five days of hostilities, a golden forty-eight hours that stretches before us like an endless glittering carpet of possibility, would seem at first glance to be enjoyed only by those of working age. You'd think that those who had trudged through the trenches of work for decades would have shaken off the spell of Friday and would have safely withdrawn from the drug of anticipating that golden child of the weekdays, but no, such is the captivation of Friday and the imprint it makes over a lifetime that older people, although unshackled from work, still continue to thrill as Friday evening approaches.

Whatever activity they conduct during the week and even if they conduct none, older survivors of the workplace are still likely to think of the fifth day of the week as a feel-good day and regard Friday as being like the relief of removing high heels or other power-dressing accessories that become redundant by the weekend. That is to assume such accoutrements were even being worn in the first place as casual dress on Fridays has long been common in many workplaces and corporate environments. There are so many possible ways to spend this superhero of the weekdays that it is virtually impossible to describe or prescribe the perfect Friday. Many will have their idealised Fridays, which might include staying in to read, watching television or burning candles while others replenish their energy by boarding the welcome wagon to the weekend and going out to celebrate. Friday is astrologically influenced by Venus, the Roman goddess of love, sensuality and connection and can therefore be an excellent night for older romantics to ply their charms on a suitably receptive object of their affections. Being replete with the energy of friendliness and kindness, Friday represents the optimal date night. The famous British rock band The Cure penned a paean to Friday's associations with the amorously entitled 'Friday I'm In Love'. The song was a worldwide hit in 1992. It is indeed not hard to see why the day was so brilliantly lauded in the lyrics of the song. However, soaking up too much alcohol on a Friday night can interfere with more lecherous ambitions, and not just in older folk. Life and beer are similar in that chilling produces best results. To avoid a tragic confidence-battering underperformance or an episode of dis-inhibited bad judgement, one is best advised to clamp shut the beer pipeline earlier rather than later on a Friday night. It may be truly satisfying for members of an older generation to rebel against the stereotypes and social rules that dictate they should always remain calm, dignified and sober, but the wrath of the grapes, in the form of an inevitable and punishing hangover, may turn the long-craved-for weekend into misery.

Alcohol, in fact, has a very long association with Friday as workers traditionally were frequently paid in public houses, to the consternation of their spouses and hungry families at the end of the working week. The joy of payday and the illusion of being rich for the day is not the sole preserve of the gainfully employed, however, as older people often receive their pensions on Fridays. The temptation to spend all one's weekly earnings on Friday is indeed typical of this roller-coaster day, and when this leaves meagre resources for the rest of the week, the view that alcohol should be regarded as man's worst enemy is understandable. The problem is that, for those looking to justify such reckless behaviour, the sermon on the following Sunday will ironically call upon them to love their enemy, unwittingly endorsing their affection for the devil's buttermilk and providing even more reason to thank God for the famous weekly 'F word'. The trick is not to just stagger from one weekend or one Friday to the next but to draw on other things we associate with the day. This may be a lot easier for the older generation who remembers the link with fasting and abstinence, a time when meat was banned from any self-respecting, God-fearing family's dinner table. For Christians, who mark the death of Jesus on Good Friday, the day is also associated with sacrifice and sombre reflection. For Friday apologists who attempt to justify and excuse Friday's delinquent traits, it seems as if Christianity has fought back at the very suggestion that any day other than Sunday ought to be celebrated.

Ultimately, Friday is a day to prepare for the take-off of the weekend, when we detoxify ourselves of the stress, the obligations and the punishment meted out during the week. For worker bees, it is the perfect antidote to a recurring Monday, but in truth it is a day like any other to those in retirement, who may now regard each and every day as a gift without discrimination. It would be interesting to know, however, how many older people, having kept all of their receipts for Post-Retirement Mondays, would still exchange them for Frivolous Fridays.

Conclusion

I hope the mixture of humorous anecdotes about ageing, combined with sombre sermons about how we should look after ourselves and change our society to embrace ageing has shown you that growing older is first and foremost a chance to do just that – grow. The greatest triumph of humanity that has the ability to affect each and every one of us in the course of hopefully long lives has been the improvement in life expectancy. This improvement allows us to reach our full potential as members of the human family. We do not have to achieve everything overnight, or at a precocious age, or when we are at our physical peak, or when we are most externally attractive to others. The attributes most associated with the older psyche such as wisdom and balance allow us to reflect on life goals and priorities to see if they still fit with our higher motives or current station in life, and if they do, the time-honoured attributes of spirit and resilience can still carry us over the line as we finally attain our destiny. I hope that you, the reader, will take up the challenge of living your later life to the fullest possible extent, that you will actively see possibilities, not just problems, and keep changing, growing and developing your unique personhood in the process of your journey.

ABOUT THE AUTHOR

Dr Declan Lyons is a consultant psychiatrist at St. Patrick's Mental Health Services in Dublin. As a physician and psychiatrist, he has over twenty years' experience working with acutely ill older people. He is a clinical senior lecturer in Psychiatry at Trinity College Dublin and has clinical and research interests in education, ethical issues in medical practice and rehabilitation of older people experiencing mental health difficulties. He is a director of Aware, the national organisation for the support of persons experiencing depression, is chair of the board of the Human Givens Institute in the United Kingdom, is Ireland representative of the Doctors Against Forced Organ Harvesting network and is an active member of Amnesty International. Along with colleagues in St. Patrick's Hospital, he contributed to and edited *The Evergreen Guide: Helping People to Survive and Thrive in Later Years*, which was published by Nova Science Publishers in New York in 2014. The book details a group-based psychological rehabilitation programme available to older inpatients in St. Patrick's Hospital. Although he is actively enjoying the middle years of his life, he aspires to reach retirement, spend his pension and become his own role model for active and successful ageing. He has written articles on healthy ageing that have been published in the heath supplement of the *Irish Times*. He is married with two children and lives in Dublin.